BLOCK
THE
PLATE

M.E. Gilbert

BLOCK THE PLATE
M.E. Gilbert

Copyright © 2014 by M.E. GIlbert
HGP Press
978-0-9894310-0-2

for my mother

CONTENTS

1

T he baseball pops off the bat – sailing fast and far, headed for deep center field. The runner waits on third so he can tag up as soon as Butch catches the ball (and believe me, Butch *will* catch that ball). I throw off my catcher's mask and get ready. The parents in the stands rise slowly, whispering "c'mon...c'mon..." Coach Manton yells at the top of his lungs. The other team holds on to their dugout fence, hoping...

Backed up almost to the warning track, Butch catches it and with his cannon of an arm makes the throw – bypassing the cut-off man, trying to get that ball to travel some three hundred feet faster than this runner barreling towards me can make it from third to home. My heartbeat hammers out the microseconds as I wait.

If this runner scores, it's a tie ballgame. If I can tag him, that's three outs and we win.

The ball takes a high hop. I have to reach up and to the left a bit – and *thump*, my favorite sound: the baseball hits my mitt. I immediately lower the glove and plant my feet in position, ready for the runner to slide into me. And slide he does – no excuses, no fear, just metal cleats headed straight at me. A cloud of dust swirls up around home plate. I hold my breath, not just to keep from breathing all that dirt but waiting to hear the call. The ump watches, concentrating. The dust settles a bit. I hold up my mitt, the ball's still in it.

"You're...OUT!"

Parents in the bleachers cheer like crazy. Players on the other team let go of the dugout fence and turn toward their bench, dejected. I relax a little.

"Hustle, boys! Line up! NOW! Get a move on!" Coach Manton keeps right on yelling at the top of his lungs.

Even when we win, we're doing something wrong. In this case, I guess we're too slow lining up to shake hands with the other team. Never mind that we are at midfield waiting for the other team a full minute before they arrive.

As good as I'm feeling, I can't ignore the pain in my left shin. I don't check it out but I'm pretty sure there's a nice gash left by the cleats of that runner sliding home. Luckily our socks are maroon so the blood won't be noticeable right away.

"Great throw," I point at Butch as we wait.

"All you, Simmons, all you," he answers with a smile. Butch and I exchange a small fist bump just as the other team shows up.

"HEY!" Coach Manton's laser gaze is on me. "If I see you celebrate again, Simmons, *that's it!*"

"Yessir!"

The guys and I have wondered a few times about Manton's constant threats of "that's it." Butch says it means that's it, you'll be off the team. My buddy Louie swears Coach would never quit on any of us, especially now that we've all been playing together for three years. Quitting is, like, the absolute worst thing in the world to Coach. Giving up on the team. Or giving up on anything, for that matter. I once saw Manton run half a mile to get some little yellow piece of paper that blew out of his wallet. When he got it, he just wadded it up and stuffed it in his pocket. Said he doesn't believe in littering. So yeah, you could say the guy's tenacious. He doesn't give up.

We only have 45 minutes before it's time to warm up for the championship game. I could just grab something from concessions but my dad says he'll take me somewhere quick if I want. I say Whataburger even though I'm not super in love with fast food – or at least, I know I shouldn't be. But it's right around the corner and the Burns family goes to Whataburger a lot, which means Louie and his twin sister Livvie might be there... Livvie's practically one of the guys and we've been friends since 6th grade. Actually, a couple of times Livvie and I were more than friends, but that's ancient history.

My dad parks and pulls out his *Film Comment* magazine. I know he won't go in with me, and maybe that's part of the reason I decided to come here too. Dad wouldn't be caught eating junk food but he always seems totally fine with waiting in our beat up old Prius while I do stuff. And that's cool. He's like a perfectly acceptable parental unit and always great and everything blah-blah, but if I can keep him from going inside and talking politics with Mr. Burns, bonus points.

As soon as I walk in, Mr. and Mrs. Burns wave hello from the corner booth where they sit with their cups of coffee. Louie and Livvie are placing orders at the counter.

"If you get French fries, I'll get onion rings and we can share," Livvie tells her brother.

"No way, get your own."

"You can have one of my French fries, Livvie," I tell her. "But only one."

"Peeeeeeete!" Louie always stretches out my name and slaps me on the back. "There he is! Did you see who we play in the finals? Slammers! Not easy, man..."

Livvie gets a kids meal prize on the side. I didn't even know you could buy the toy separately. It's a pop-up frog with a suction cup bottom.

"Is Manton starting you?" I ask Louie.

"Well, hellz to the yeah!" Louie slaps my back again. "And you better be the one catching me, Simmons." He says it like a threat, as if I have any power over when I play.

Livvie pushes the suction cup down onto the counter. "Of course it'll be Pete. Manton's not going to start Jeff Bellows at catcher in the *finals*, hello," she says. The frog pops up and she catches it in mid-air.

"Oh really, Coach tell you that?" Louie puts her in a chokehold, trying to grab the frog from her. "Has he been sharing his game plan with you?"

"Do you see what I have to put up with?" she asks me.

While inhaling our burgers, Louie and I talk about the best hitters he'll be facing from the Slammers. It feels great to be in the championship game, another one under our belt. Maybe we can extend the Texas Blaze winning streak to five tournaments in a row. Louie tries to say I made a nice play on that final out today, but I tell him Butch's throw was epic and I was just there to catch it. Even though I get the glory in some of those situations, Coach Manton always teaches that we're only as good as whoever's throwing it to us.

We are sitting at our own booth across the restaurant from Mr. and Mrs. Burns. Livvie keeps popping up that frog randomly while eating most of my fries. According to her, the onion rings suck today. When Louie goes to the bathroom, I ask Livvie about the tournament she played this weekend. Livvie is a killer volleyball player, but not the tall one who can spike it. She's a libero – you know, the one who digs for those balls like crazy, throwing herself all over the floor. Once I saw her dive for a ball on the line, get to it in time and pop it upward in a perfect set – but her forward momentum carried her into a full somersault. Then she just rolled back up to a standing position and kept playing. All while the ball was live. Yeah, you could say she is pretty good.

Livvie is telling me about this parent who volunteered to be a line judge but couldn't get the arm signals straight – so every time he said "IN!" he would lift his hands in the "OUT" motion. Her impersonations are perfect, of everyone from the irritated net judge to the perplexed coaches.

"So only one more week of school." I lean back with a smile.

Soon we'd have more free time to do our sports. And maybe to see each other. You know, just to hang out. As friends. Or whatever.

"Yes! Summer!" she says. "That's what I

keep telling myself, no matter what tests they throw at us – summer's coming. And guess what? I might be getting a job."

"What job? Where?"

But she just smiles. One thing about Livvie, she's a vault when she wants to be.

"Come on, give me a hint."

"I don't want to jinx it."

"One hint?" I grab the frog in midair as it pops up. "You better tell me!"

"My froggie! Okay, okay, one hint..." And she reaches up and holds her nose.

"That's the hint?"

She nods and just keeps pinching her nose.

"Something...smelly?"

Her smile gets bigger.

"Okay, smelly, smelly, let me think...Are you working...on a garbage truck? Or babysitting?"

"Babysitting?" Livvie's voice comes out in a weird nasal tone through her pinched nose.

"You know, changing the diapers."

She sort of snorts out a laugh.

"No wait, wait, I got it!" I continue. "You're pet sitting for a skunk!"

"Because there are so many skunk sitting jobs out there."

Mr. and Mrs. Burns throw away their coffee cups and head toward the door.

"Or a port-a-pottie person?"

"What is that?" She lets go of her nose.

"Think about it. Who puts that blue dye down in there?"

"You are gross!" But her smile makes me feel anything but gross. "Anyway, I'm not telling."

Louie follows his parents outside. Through the window, I can see Mr. Burns start giving Louie a few tips on how to pitch tonight. Really helpful. Not.

I hand Livvie the plastic frog as we go out.

"Wait, what happened to your leg?" she asks.

Oh that's right. The blood has soaked through my sock and dried in a big dark stain. And I realize it does kind of hurt.

"It's okay, I'm fine."

I'm really not playing the tough guy, it's

just I know if we peel my sock down right now, it will start bleeding again and we'll have to get bandages and Mrs. Burns will probably get that fancy first aid kit out of their car and make me put some sort of painful medicine on it... Best to just wait until my shower tonight. Besides, it's time to go.

"You gotta get a bandaid or something, seriously," Livvie holds the glass door open for me. "You bled all over your leg."

"Makes me look tough."

"Tough, huh? Can I be honest?"

"No," I tell her.

She tosses me the frog toy. "Good luck in the championship," she says as she gets in her car.

2

The Triple Play Premiere Field of Dreams Complex was just built last year and the place has got serious swag, as Butch says. The tournament finals are being played on Field #1: the diamond's a little sunken, the dugout benches have backrests, the stadium lights are super bright, the outfield fence is even padded. Playing there is like real-deal nice, as good or even better than any high school field. Of course, this isn't a *high school* game, it's only 14U. Playing varsity for Welton High is the next step in the big dream hanging over all of us, and supposedly that's where our time on Texas Blaze has us headed. We hope. Making Manton's team is sort of known as the ticket to... I don't want to talk about that. I'm not superstitious or anything but why talk about something before it happens? Let's just say Manton and Welton High's Coach Smith go waaaaay back.

Anyway, Triple Play Field of Dreams is fantastic, except for one thing. The wind never stops blowing. I guess they didn't notice that when they were building it.

I spit out a mouthful of dust before I crouch back into position. I'm normally not one of those baseball players who frickin' hock one every time you turn around. I mean, I'm not against it or anything but I just don't have a bucket of extra saliva spontaneously forming in my mouth. I used to actually *try* and spit when I was in Little League in East Austin. Everybody did, it was a cool grown-up kind of thing to do back then. There was this kid Julio who used to be able to land his spit on any sunflower seed shell you wanted – he had aim, man! I'm serious, it was amazing. I once lost a brand new package of bubble gum tape to him, betting he couldn't spit over the bench and land on a penny. Dumb bet, he got it on the first try. I haven't thought about that guy Julio in years – I knew him back before we moved. Now I live in Welton Heights and play real baseball, where there's not as much time to fool around in the dugout. Besides, Coach Manton would flip.

We get two outs quickly, then Louie walks a guy. I reposition my mask and settle behind the plate. Manton gives me a fast ball signal, and I give Louie the sign and he nods quickly. The batter steps into the box – a rightie whose hands are shaking. I don't know him, even though we've already played the Slammers in several tournaments this spring. This kid must be new, maybe just moved up from one of their other teams. They are a big organization and the Slammers have had some injuries, unlike us. The Texas Blaze haven't had any real injuries all spring. Knock wood.

This guy's bat is even new – the latest Easton, with barely a scratch on it. This is the $349.95 XL1 model, I know because Louie was just showing it to me on his phone yesterday. He wants one for his birthday next month. And knowing Mr. and Mrs. Burns, I'd doubt he'll even have to wait that long.

Not super fast, but the ball comes straight down the middle. Louie must've also noticed this guy was nervous and decided to freeze him with an easy pitch. Risky, but it pays off.

"Strike!" is yelled just behind my head. I love enthusiastic umps. Unless I'm on the wrong side of the call, of course.

Louie's next pitch is just what Coach has told me to signal: low and outside. It works, and the newbie lunges awkwardly for it. The ball lands in my worn mitt with a satisfying smack.

"O and two, o and two now," calls the Slammers coach from his third base box. "Be-a-hitter. Anything-close. Rally-here. Protect-the-plate. Be-a-hitter. C'mon-now."

I don't know about you, but one of the things I love about baseball is all the chatter. Yeah, everybody's stating the obvious. "O and two...be a hitter." We all know the count is no balls, two strikes. We all want to be hitters. But it's the rhythm, you know what I mean? Like the singsong lilt when girls used to jump rope at recess...or at least the girls at my elementary school back in East Austin used to do that. I don't know why but I just like to hear a dozen or more people all stating the obvious and backing you up, urging you on. It helps sometimes. It's the background noise that gets you in the zone. It's iTunes while you do homework. It's SportsCenter while you eat breakfast. It's listening to your headphones on the way to the game. It's the soundtrack to the movie of your life... JK on that last one. I'm not that corny. But just because it's corny doesn't mean it's not true. Wow, did I just quote my mom? "Just because it's corny, doesn't mean it's not true, Pete."

Anyway, what I'm trying to say is a quiet at-bat is usually a bad at-bat. But sometimes even chatter can't help you.

I look to Coach Manton for the sign, figuring he'll call another fast ball outside. Nope, he wants to brush this guy back. Really? Okay, Coach...

I give Louie the sign and I can tell he's a little surprised too, but of course we don't question it or even glance at the dugout. There's no such thing as shaking off one of Manton's calls. I get ready to frame it, and Louie steps on the rubber, taking quick glances at the runner on base over his shoulder. From the stretch, he delivers quick...and bounces it in front of the plate.

The ball takes a bad hop and goes flying

right past me. The runner at first makes it to second and a little beyond by the time I throw off my mask and find the ball back by the fence. The Slammers coach is calling his runner, waving him to third. I set my feet beneath me as best I can in that half a second and fire the ball to Richard, our third baseman. I throw as fast and straight as I know how.

I see Richard tense up. He's good, but he never plays loose, you know what I mean? I think it's because Richard's never played a position where he gets a lot of regular contact with the ball (pitcher, catcher, first base) so he's always half scared when he sees it coming his way. I mean, he can react fast and do it well – when he doesn't have to think about it. Like when a line drive comes screaming off the bat straight toward him, then Richard will usually stick his glove out on instinct and catch it no problem. That makes him a perfect third baseman. But this is different – one of those moments when you see the runner heading toward you and you have to get set, get ready to react. I think those few extra milliseconds of anticipation kind of do Richard in.

Or maybe it's those few extra milliseconds to worry about how his dad is going to yell at him later.

The ball is coming in low and right, the perfect position for him to catch and tag the runner as he slides. Richard catches it clean and holds his position as the runner slides. Yes! Nice! Why was I worried? When the dust clears, Richard holds up his glove to show that he has the ball – and drops it.

"Safe!"

You've got to be kidding me.

I see Coach Manton inside the dugout, glaring at me.

Is he blaming me? He always says, *You're only as good as whoever's throwing it to you...*

I can't let him get in my head right now. But really, is Manton mad at me? What could I have done better? My dad always says the best players are the ones coaches yell at the most. If that's true, I must be headed for the Hall of Fame.

Back to the batter. Forget everything else. Concentrate. It's one and two now. One ball, two strikes. Pitcher's count.

But Coach still has the same idea, he wants to brush this guy back. Why, I have no idea since the kid's probably not going to swing at anything, but I'm rattled by that last play at third and I   just go with it. I mean, what else can I do but go with it? I think fast-ball-right-down-the-middle would be an easy strike with this count and this batter, but what do I know.

I give Louie the signal and maybe he doesn't know what I'm saying or maybe he thinks it's a bad idea too, but this time Louie throws the high and outside, just missing the corner of the plate.

"Ball!"

Count's even, 2-2, but Manton again wants the brush back. And again I signal it and again Louie seems to ignore it...

Another low and outside – only this time newbie swings. Turns out he loves the out-side ball. And for good reason. We all watch it go about one inch over that fancy padded fence in right center, landing somewhere in the cow pasture beyond.

I see Louie punch his fist into his glove a few times and put his chin down to his chest. I think about running out to the mound and giving him an *atta boy* but another batter steps up and I don't think Louie's in the mood to talk anyway. I crouch back down and one of my straps comes undone. I have to call time to reconnect my shin guards. I can feel Coach Manton pacing in the dugout but I don't look his way.

"Doing great guys, just keep playing!" My dad in the stands with his optimism. I feel my face get even warmer.

Funny how when you're ahead, the whole world is great. Jokes are funny, your water jug is full and cold, your shoes are never untied. But when the team's behind, everything changes. Grit blows in your eyes, the umps make bad calls, and your cup is the most uncomfortable thing in the universe.

Jees, I *cannot* get this leg strap to stay hooked!

If Richard hadn't dropped that ball at third, we would've already been out of this inning. And then this new kid wouldn't have hit it out of the park on his first-ever at bat with the Slammers, which will no doubt be a huge confidence boost for him and a lifelong memory. Now this newbie will probably become known as a slugger and get moved higher in the line up. And with his team and coach behind him, he'll start to believe in himself. And you know what, that will probably *make* him a good hitter. This from the kid who was standing in front of me, quaking, less than a minute ago. Now he's frickin' Miguel Cabrera.

That's the thing maybe some people don't realize about baseball: at any given moment, a game can go off in a bunch of directions. Every little thing affects all that happens forward. It's the road not taken, but times about a thousand, with every play. Sometimes I imagine a baseball game with all its other possible variations branching out. The might-have-been outcomes... When coaches and ex-players and TV announcers talk about how baseball is like life, I think that's what they mean. It can all change completely in every at-bat. With every pitch.

And it does. For better or worse.

So on this day in history, Newbie got a hitter's reputation and we lost, 1-2.

Hello, second place.

"None of you were prepared for the kind of game we faced today." Coach Manton paces as we hang our heads and gulp from our dusty water jugs, wiping the sticky sweat from our brows.

Whenever we win, it seems like Coach can usually find a shady spot for us to sit and hear his post-game speech. When we lose, we find ourselves squatting in a hot parking lot or the middle of a wide sunny sidewalk, with pedestrians navigating around, most of them unable to avoid hearing Manton bawl us out.

"And you Simmons!"

I straighten up. I try to have no expression on my face, because there isn't a right one to have.

"Outside pitches? Two in a row? What are you thinking?! What are you DOING? That's not what I called!"

I know to even glance at Louie would be giving him up. That would mean I'm a disloyal teammate, which is even worse than giving the pitcher the wrong sign.

"And don't blame it on Lou!" Coach kicks my baseball bag for emphasis. It bangs into my cut shin pretty hard, but I don't react at all. Or at least I try not to.

"Lou is the pitcher, he throws what you call! This is your game, this is your field, these are your players! I tell you what to call and you call it!" By now Coach is breathing down my neck, daring me to react. "You hear me, Simmons?!"

A little voice inside me says, if this is my game and my field, why is Coach telling me what to call? But I just shout out "Yessir!" mechanically.

21

"Did you see my signs, Simmons?"

"Yessir!"

"Pete Simmons...you're telling me...you saw the signs...for high and inside?"

What am I supposed to say? I know he's leading me into a trap.

"Yessir!"

He squats next to me, and takes a deep breath.

"Then tell me something, Simmons..." His voice is barely a whisper. Everyone on the team holds his breath. "Why did we have two low outside pitches in a row?"

Now here is a tricky moment. If I say 'I don't know,' then he'll jump down my throat. If I give any sort of excuse or reasoning, he'll jump down my throat. If I blame it on Louie, Coach will jump down my throat. And then he'll jump down Louie's throat.

The question hangs in the air.

A mom and dad with a couple of little toddlers walk around us. "Base-ball!" says the youngest, looking at us.

"That's right, Braden!" says his dad. "Baseball! Big boy baseball players!"

Louie has the nerve to look up and smile

at that little kid. When the boy waves, Louie waves back. Out of the corner of his eye, Coach Manton sees this happen.

Coach takes another deep breath and stares at the ground until the family with the little kids has walked on past. I swear I can see a vein pumping on the side of his head. I try not to look.

"Burns! Did you shake off Simmons' signs?!"

And so it goes, now Louie's turn to be the focus of wrath. Coach Manton takes his time, blaming the defeat on almost every guy there. Flat-Top didn't have his head in the game. Butch didn't throw that pop fly in fast enough to make a double play. Brady struck out looking. We are all major screw-ups, according to Coach Manton. But amazingly, Coach never says a word to Richard for dropping the ball at third. I mean, if there was a key moment when an error really cost us the game, most people would point to that. Not that any game ever comes down to one play.

Everyone knows Richard's dad owns Loezier's Jewelry Stores. Yeah, that Loezier's Jewelry – the one in your local mall. And every other mall in America, just about. Richard Loezier is super rich, even by the standards of

Welton Heights. He goes to St. Anthony's which is the best private school in town, and he has a house in Sun Valley and a house in Florida and a house in someplace-else-I-can't-remember, with a helicopter landing pad at every one of them. And guess what? He is actually a really super nice guy. Everybody likes Richard. And absolutely no one envies him. Because no one wants Mr. Loezier for a dad.

Speak of the devil, Mr. Loezier is waiting for Richard as soon as the post-game huddle breaks up. I take off across the parking lot, where I spot the old Prius with all its bumperstickers. Even though I'm not looking at Richard, I can hear his dad yelling at him. The word "idiot" comes through loud and clear as I shut the passenger door.

"Hungry?" my dad greets me.

My dad's Italian. When times are bad, he likes to eat. When times are good, he likes to eat even more. Win or lose, a salami sub is usually what the doctor ordered.

"And that thing's been buzzing." Dad points to my phone, stuck in a cup holder.

It's a text from Livvie: *Remember – summer's coming!*

3

Even on the last day of school, I get up early to do sit-ups and push-ups before my shower. For Christmas, my Uncle Luke came to town and made me a chin-up bar. It was really cool, right in the doorway of my closet, but it broke after a few weeks. I'm going to try and fix it one of these days. If I can borrow some tools from somebody. And if they show me how to use the tools. On second thought, maybe I'll just wait for Uncle Luke to come back to town. My dad's great but he's not exactly handy and I've never really learned how to build things either.

By the time I get out of the shower, I hear my parents making coffee downstairs. I shuffle through my drawers, looking for a pair of socks with no holes in them. I have to wear one each from two different pairs, but they are almost the same shade of blue. The cut on my shin is pretty much healed up.

"Last day!" my mom leans in the doorway and watches me tie my shoes.

"Uh huh."

"Middle school is already over, can you believe it? Almost a high school freshman..." She closes my sock drawer and straightens the stack of textbooks. She starts to put the books back on the shelf.

"Mom, wait – I have to turn those back in today." I go to grab them and see her wipe away a tear.

I give her a little hug and I guess that makes her wipe away a few more tears.

"Since when do I not come up to your shoulder?!" She holds me tight. "I swear, an inch a week here lately. So tall!"

"No, Mom, you're just shrinking. That happens to old people sometimes."

She play-slaps at me but I jump out of the way.

"French toast?" she says.

"I could maybe force it down." I evade her hand again.

French toast sounds really good. And just think, as of this afternoon, it is *summer*. Long empty days to play baseball and go to the pool and sleep and play xBox and then play more baseball...

My backpack is overstuffed with all those heavy textbooks and when I put it down on the kitchen bar, it rips. "Oh man..."

My mom sprinkles a little powdered sugar over my plate of toast. "You'll need a new one for high school next year anyway."

Dad examines the backpack. "Some duct tape would fix this up."

My mom and I exchange a look.

"What?" he protests. "I meant on the inside, I'd tape it on the inside. It wouldn't be visible!"

"Okay, sure honey..." My mom winks at me.

"Reduce, reuse, recycle," I chime in.

"Exactly!" Dad's eyes light up.

"Don't encourage him," says Mom.

There is a party atmosphere at school.

Teachers tear things off their bulletin boards and play music in the classrooms. Girls are wearing shorts that don't exactly meet dress code as they sign yearbooks with lip-gloss kisses. Butch and I sit on top of a picnic table in the courtyard, even though normally the vice principal would come tell us that we have to keep our "behinds on the benches." Today the rules are lax. We are graduates.

Thursday night there was a little graduation ceremony, with kids waiting in line to have the principal hand them rolled-up diplomas (turned out to be just blank paper tied with a ribbon, you got the real thing later). My friends and I had skipped it. We had baseball practice as an excuse, but I'd doubt we would have gone anyway. I hear that ceremony is sort of a dweeby thing for people who don't have anything but grades in their life. Except Livvie went, apparently. She is one of those people who crosses a lot of lines and is hard to pin down to any one identity. Mine is simple: I am a jock. A baseball jock, to be exact. And I am fine with that. It's a lot better than what I used to be three years ago: a poor transfer student.

When I was about to start sixth grade, my parents had this sort of crisis where they decided in a panic that I couldn't go to the middle school in my old neighborhood. Apparently there had been a kid with a gun there. Or was it drugs? Or maybe both, now that I think about it. Anyway, I never got all the details and Dad always said it was a *perfectly good school* but Mom insisted on applying for this transfer. When I got in, she was so relieved. Eventually my folks sold our house in East Austin and rented a duplex in these western suburbs so I could always be assured a spot in the high-rated schools. And I'm really glad they did. Because if not, I'd never have gotten to play on the Texas Blaze and meet all of the guys. Or even Livvie for that matter.

Livvie leans across me now, showing iPhone photos of last night's graduation to Butch: there are various people getting their diplomas, eating slices of grocery-store cake, posing with their arms around each other, making funny faces – pooched out lips and peace signs.

"Wow, so many people went..." says Butch.

"Everybody was there, except you guys!" says Livvie. "I can't believe Coach M wouldn't cancel practice! That's like, wrong!"

I can smell Livvie's shampoo or perfume

or lotion or whatever it is. Flowery and lemony. It's kinda nice. It's familiar. Funny how things like a certain smell you can forget and not even think about until you come across it again. I hadn't been really close to this fragrance too many times, but I'd been practically knocked out by it on the couple of times Livvie and I had kissed. Yeah, that's right. Kissed. Three times, actually. At the end of sixth grade at Kayla Jenkin's birthday party when I was sort of pulling Livvie around on a skateboard out on the driveway, that was the first time. The second was when a bunch of us had "double dated" in 7th grade and gone to a scary movie. Everybody was kissing their "girlfriends" and Livvie and I sort of had to go along with it. That had been no fun – I hate scary movies and the whole thing was just so forced and on display and nerve-wracking. One girl was taking pictures with her phone and some weird adults sitting a few rows down kept shushing us and the whole thing was stupid.

But the third time had been after the Blaze had beat Los Alamos in the Slugfest Fall Series championship game. That was such a cool tournament, definitely the highlight of 7th grade. They actually gave out rings that said "Slugfest Fall Champions" and looked like a class ring with a big ruby red stone in it... Coach Manton even got one, and he wore it proudly for weeks. And he had smiled. That in itself was like a miracle or something.

After that Slugfest game, the whole team had gone to Rudy's Barbecue. We sat at long wooden tables and ate ribs and brisket off pieces of white waxed paper and drank root beer. Coach Manton gave a speech about how his game plan had worked to perfection and if we kept adhering to it, the sky was the limit. Even Richard's mom was there that night, laughing and talking. And of course, Livvie came.

After stuffing ourselves on smoked meat, we left all the parents inside and went to play touch football on a patch of grass they have behind the restaurant. That's probably the reason most families go to that place, actually. The food is pretty good but my dad says it's not as good as the little bbq shacks in East Austin. Whatever. I love Rudy's, because kids can go out back while the parents sit around and shoot the bull.

Louie and I were appointed QBs, and he got the ball first. Louie passed and Butch intercepted and scored. We were already winning 6-0. Nice. Next play, Louie throws again – this time to his sister. Livvie caught it and ran, but I went as fast as my legs would take me and two-hand-touched her.

"Okay, first down! Give me the ball, Livvie!" Louie shouted.

Livvie tossed the ball to her twin brother in a perfect spiral. The teams huddled up, but before we could join them, Livvie pulled me toward the woods.

"Come on!"

"What about the game?" I looked over my shoulder, but no one seemed to miss us. "I'm quarterback."

I had to admit it was a pretty loose contest. Richard was doing standing back flips and a couple of little brothers were trying to tackle Butch, to no avail.

As we walked into a shadowy spot under a tree, Livvie touched my arm. "You're it!" And she ran.

Instinctively, I gave chase. With all the trees and the dark, she was hard to catch! I mean, I was actually really trying and I just could not tag her. Finally she stepped out in the clear and waited.

"Couldn't catch me, huh?" Her eyes sparkled, pale blue.

"I wasn't trying."

"Yeah, right!" She gave my shoulder a push.

I stepped closer and she stepped closer, and somehow we were kissing.

"Simmons? Simmons, hellooooo!"

I jump back to reality, sitting on the picnic table in the commons on the last day of 8th grade.

"Hey, what's up?" I nod at Butch.

He and Livvie both laugh.

"Earth to Pete," says Liv, and gives me one of her goofy faces.

Livvie and I are good friends now, and all of that kissing stuff is ancient history. A couple of weeks after that night at Rudy's, I had asked Livvie if it was kind of awkward being boyfriend/girlfriend seeing as her brother was my friend and all of that...She jumped on that so quickly, I barely got to say anything else – she blurted out that it was all too much pressure and she agreed that the idea of going steady was *stupid*. Well. I guess that was what I had been thinking too...in a way.

"You were zoning out there!" Livvie nudges me with her shoulder.

"Sorry..." I want to tell her I was remembering the past, or something like that, but of course I can't.

"He was probably staring at Alicia!" Butch says in a too-loud whisper.

Alicia Caldwell is across the courtyard, with a long line of people patiently waiting to have her sign their yearbook. She is the official "prettiest girl" in our grade, although I think that all of her make up and pointy shoes and fashion-type clothes are kind of silly. She always looks uncomfortable, but I think she is just a regular person under there.

Right at that second, Alicia looks up and waves to us with manicured fingernails. To be polite I wave back.

"Well, I should go!" Livvie hops off the table.

"Oh, you...uh...okay..." I say. Real smooth.

As Livvie walks away, she pumps her fist. "High school, here we come!"

4

It's the first day of summer and the first tournament of our official summer season. It's just a quick one day tourney, where it's all pool play and they rank you by games won, runs allowed, etc. It's just a chance for us to get warmed up for the big travel tournaments we have scheduled.

And after our first game, the Texas Blaze have their first official loss of the official summer season. Did not see that coming. Not the way we were planning to start.

Manton is always real big on working hard in the face of adversity, but the thing is – usually we don't have any adversity. The

Blaze are known for winning. Anyway, today he doesn't give any of his speeches on working through difficulties or anything like that. He just scowls and snaps at us for things we can't control. I guess he's pretty upset, and maybe he should be. I can't remember the last time we lost two games in a row, even with a week in between the losses. This is not good.

To their credit, the other team is fantastic. The Bandidos. They're from the Houston area and don't travel up here too often, so we'd been dying to play them. Or so we thought. To tell you the truth, now I am sort of glad that they don't come here much. The Bandidos must have five guys who are over six feet tall. I usually hate when some of the parents joke around and say things like, "I wanna see his birth certificate!" but this time, I am almost agreeing with them. One of the Bandidos pitchers has a mustache. I mean a real, actual, complete mustache.

Anyway, next up is game two. We'll have to claw our way back up to the top. No problem, the Blaze has done that before.

I get into the Prius, where my dad is doing a crossword puzzle.

"Oh good, you're here. The bird in Froot

Loops ads? Let's see...seven, eight, nine letters."

"Toucan Sam. Duh."

"Nice!" He writes it in, then starts the car. "You hungry? How about Pizza Bistro?"

"We have to be back in two hours."

"Oh..." Dad puts his foot on the brake. "I thought the next game was at—"

"Coach wants us back early."

"Got it. Subway, then!"

He heads toward the nearby sandwich shop. He knows places to eat around every baseball field in Central Texas, I think.

I pick up my phone and see a text from Livvie: HOW MUCH U WIN BY? Followed by one of those tiny smiley faces with the tongue sticking out.

Even though getting that text is probably the best thing that's happened so far today, I still don't feel like texting back just to tell her we lost. I put my phone down. I'll text her after we win the next game.

I lean back and watch the pastures full of cedar trees turn into a small town's main street. I stayed up way too late last night celebrating the last day of summer by playing xBox at Richard Loezier's. He has it hooked up to this gigantic TV that is so big, it makes the game, like, addictive. But now the late night is hitting me and I regret playing MLB 2K so late. And even after we went to bed, I couldn't sleep in Richard's giant high-ceilinged bedroom. I close my eyes as we speed along.

"You stay out here and rest, I'll get it to go."

Next thing I know, Dad has parked the car and is getting out.

Through the window of Subway, I can see Butch and Louie laughing. They seem not to care that we just lost. I envy that. But I can't afford to relax like that. If I don't win baseball games, I don't have too much going for me.

"That'd be great, Dad. Thanks." I recline my seat even further and close my eyes again.

"Sure thing, bud."

Bud.

When I played my first year of Little League baseball, my dad coached me. He could never remember all the boys' names so he called them all "bud." My mom had talked him into coaching since he played in high school and loved the game and all that. It was coach pitch, which is halfway between tee ball and regular rules. It means the coaches have to pitch to their own players since the kids aren't old enough to throw strikes, but are too big to hit it off a tee. At least that was the prevailing thought. My dad says you are never too old to hit it off a tee.

But back to Little League coach pitch: it turns out my dad could basically hit any kid's bat, if they would just hold it out there. It's like some weird mutant skill he has. Our team wound up winning it all that year, because no one ever struck out. We all just learned to hold our bats out very carefully and Dad would hit them with the ball. Other teams caught on, but instead of complaining they just asked him to pitch to their team, too. So there was my dad kneeling in the middle of a Little League field, lobbing it toward a bunch of six-year-olds' unsteady metal bats every Saturday morning. He said he liked it, and I think he did. But he never coached again.

Ever since then, he doesn't get too involved in my baseball stuff. He does give me advice sometimes though. For instance?

Don't take advice. Well, something along those lines: that I should at least think it over and see if I believe in it or if it feels right. Yeah, my dad says things like, "See if it feels right, bud." His hair is slightly longer than the other dads. He teaches Film Studies at the community college, which is sort of a weird job. I mean it's not like being an investment banker or building subdivisions. Or owning Loezier's Jewelers. But Livvie thinks it's cool. She loves movies.

My mom is the one with the fulltime job – she is a librarian in East Austin. She first started there when I was really little, and it was this new fancy library the city built in the middle of this crummy neighborhood. But now people are starting to buy houses around there and fix them up. Mom says she wants to move back over as soon as I graduate. They're ready to quit renting the Suburban Dream Home, as they sarcastically refer to our duplex. Just four more years and I'll be out of high school. My sister already graduated. She's at Sarah Lawrence, up in New York. My parents are so proud, but I hear them talking about how expensive it is even though they qualified for a bunch of student aid. Maybe I can get a baseball scholarship so my college won't cost them as much.

That's my secret plan, although I'd never say it out loud to them. It's so far away. Still, how nice would that be? A scholarship. Step one is making the high school team so let's not get ahead of ourselves.

I wake up to the ding-ding-ding the car makes as my dad opens the door. I eat my sandwich on the way back to the field. I put on my headphones and click my pre-game playlist, starting to get mentally ready to play. My favorite song vibrates down into my bones and I am excited to get back out on the field.

The pumped-up energy of those songs has completely faded by the time we are down 6-2 and on our way deeper into the loser's bracket. Our whole team is in a bad mood. Even Butch is subdued. We squeak out of the inning with a couple of Ks from the bottom of their line-up and now we are up. Our last at bat. Need four runs to tie, five to win. I'm leading off.

"Come on guys, let's do this!" Louie tries to get everybody going.

I put on my batting helmet and get my bat. I don't wear batting gloves, I've never gotten in the habit. Everyone else does, but that is one of those things that doesn't "feel right" as my dad would say, so I never wear them.

"Yeah, let's go! Rally!" Richard flips his cap inside out and puts it back on. We can always count on Richard for some team spirit. He throws his head back and hoots. That gets a smile out of Butch. Bellows turns his hat into a rally cap too, backwards on his head.

Here we go!

Coach is pacing outside the dugout, even more keyed up than usual.

"Ball in!" calls the ump. I take a few practice swings. That buzz of the bat cutting through the air makes hair on the back of my neck stand up a little. I'll never get tired of the sensation of swinging for the fences. Zzzzhhhup! Zzzzhhhup! This bat feels good, balanced but heavy. I moved up to a drop three this year, 32" and 29 ounces. It's a little too long and is a couple of years old, but still the best bat I've ever had. My mom found it on Craigslist for forty bucks, a used Demarini from somebody who must've outgrown it or something. I can't imagine why they'd sell it for so cheap. I retaped the handle so it feels (and looks) new and I only use it in games. My old 6th grade bat is what I pull out for BP. Coach says we should always be "game ready" and use the same bat all the time, so I don't tell him. I'm always hoping he won't notice the different bats and so far he hasn't.

"Simmons! Batter up, boy!" he yells my way. During games and practices, the guys and I always joke we are on CMT – Coach Manton Time. He hates dawdling. There are no allowances for getting your head right, no pauses for mental preparation or even untied shoes. It is step up and swing. Step up and pitch. Go, go, go. Butch says Coach Manton should've gone into basketball. Too bad he hates all sports except baseball.

"Let's go, Pete! Here you go, bat to ball, let's go..." my teammates start in with their chants and cheers.

Zzzzhhhup! The feel of the bat zipping through the air isn't so great when you are waiting for the *ping* of the ball.

"Steeee-rike one!"

I step out of the box and take a deep breath.

The guys in the dugout call, "Now you're ready!...Nicc cut, Pete...Here we go, Simmons...That wasn't your ball...You got this...Right here, right now!"

My teammates have my back.

Coach Manton paces in my peripheral vision. This pitcher is a guy I know from a baseball camp a couple of years ago, some whiz kid who was a foot taller than everyone in 5th grade but then quit growing. Most of us have caught up with him by now, or even surpassed him. These days, a lot of us can probably hit him fairly easily but that doesn't stop him from being cocky. He still has the chest-out strut of someone accustomed to winning. I remember him striking me out three different times that camp. He went home with the Junior Cy Young ribbon. I take another practice swing and tell myself that was a long time ago. I step back into the batter's box.

A dark cloud goes across the sun and I can see the ball perfectly as it comes toward me. Low and outside, just like I like it. He must think I don't have a chance, giving me that. I'm not going to look a gift horse in the mouth. *PING*. It feels good. It feels right. I wish I could just stand there and watch the ball climb and soar, but of course I have to drop my bat and take off. Speed is one of the "plus" marks in my skill set. Coach Manton is always distributing these "Scouting Reports" that he writes up on all of us. That sounds kind of good, right? Until you realize he distributes everybody's report to every player. I hate reading the negative things about myself almost as much as I hate reading them about my teammates. It's like a car wreck, you can't look away. One time Butch got tears in his eyes when Manton wrote about him being fat. That's actually the word Coach used. Fat. But Butch did wind up losing some weight, so I guess it worked.

I round second and see Manton waving me on, circling his arm in its socket like a madman. I dig and keep going. I can't believe my ball isn't in yet, but I don't dare look to see what is happening. My job is to keep my eyes on Coach and nothing else, just do what he says.

"HOLD UP, HOLD UP, HOLD UP!!" Manton yells when I am already ten feet past third base and headed full speed for home. I throw the brakes on best I can, but I'm halfway there by the time I turn back for third. I dive headfirst but the throw beats me by a mile.

"You're out!" the infield ump calls, I think with a tiny note of apology in his voice already. I know that ump, and I know he is well aware of Manton's reputation for tirades.

"WHAT ARE YOU DOING?" Manton takes off his cap and throws it on the ground in fury. "I said hold up, goddamnit!" His whole body seems to tremble, almost ready to pounce.

I disentangle myself from the third baseman and straighten my batting helmet.

"What the hell are you thinking?!" As I stand up, Manton is in my face, huffing and spitting in red-faced anger. "Why I put you at lead off, I'll never know!"

I walk toward the dugout. Everyone in the stands looks away from me or, worse, gives me a smile of pity. There is one vaguely familiar old man glaring at me. I'm not sure who he is, but he wears a Texas Blaze hat and he looks like he wants to punch me. His eyes never leave me as I make the walk of shame from third base.

Richard meets me at the dugout entrance with a pat on the back. "Get 'em next time, bro."

"Louie! Batter up!!" Manton yells from his third base box, even though the pitcher isn't ready. The other team is still throwing the ball around the infield to celebrate the out.

The dark cloud above starts to sprinkle.

It's our last game of the day and we still don't have a W. After six innings, we have eked out a lead of 11-10 and it is pouring rain, but Coach won't let them stop the game. I mean technically, if they called the game at this point on account of weather it would be a win for us. But Manton doesn't like to quit anything, ever. Quitting is the cardinal sin for him.

A crack of lightning in the distance causes the homeplate umpire to actually halt the game, but Manton goes out and has a "discussion" with him. They bring over the other coach, who of course wants to keep playing so maybe they can win. All the fields around us are emptying out and people are dashing to their cars to wait out the downpour.

"Batter up!" the ump yells.

Next thing you know, we are back out on the diamond in the middle of a thunderstorm. I hear some of the parents grumbling and wondering about safety, but none of them comes over to confront Coach Manton. They just huddle under the concession stand awning, watching and complaining.

Three more outs and we are out of here. C'mon, let's get three.

Richard pitches to three batters. And walks three batters. Bases loaded, no outs. Of course, Manton visits the mound.

"How are you feeling, Loezier?" Coach asks Richard.

Richard tries to hand the ball over to Manton, knowing he doesn't have a chance of getting out of this inning, but Coach doesn't take the ball.

"You wanna give it another try?" Coach asks, all patient-like.

"Just don't have it in the tank today, sorry Coach," says Richard.

Coach nods and finally takes the baseball. Then points to Louie. "Burns!"

Louie trots over. He already pitched a complete game this morning but Coach always says all the talk about the dangers of overuse injuries are just some trumped up BS, and if your mechanics are sound it's not a problem. And Louie never has been hurt, so obviously it's true. I guess.

As I head back to the plate, Coach shouts to me, "Simmons, nothing gets by you! Be a wall back there, you hear me?!"

Yeah, I hear you and so does everyone

else at the game. "Yessir!"

A catcher doesn't have a lot of time to react when Louie is pitching. He is fast ball after fast ball unless Coach tells me to signal something else. Louie is suddenly *on* today, and I mean completely. He is zinging them in with total assurance, and he must be topping 80 every single time. Maybe it has something to do with the storm, but usually a wet ball slows way down, right? All I know is my thumb is tingling from the force of these pitches. As fast as he is throwing, he is not completely accurate. And with the rain periodically blowing right in my face, I am struggling to keep everything in front of me. And wouldn't you know, as soon as I have that thought, one finally gets by me.

With the bases loaded, the guy on third has to run or nobody can run. And this guy on third has a big lead. He jumps toward me but stops, unsure if he should risk it. The screaming in the stands is super loud. I throw off my mask and spin around.

"To your right! To your right!" I hear my dad's voice among all the others.

But what does that mean? Because now I am facing backward, so is it to the right now or to the right of where I usually squat? Frantic, I twist around and scan the area – trying to see the ball is even harder in the rain. A flash of lightning illuminates everything for a split second – there it is, by the fence. I lunge for the ball. Louie is already covering home. The guy on third has decided to go for it. I toss the ball to Louie from my position sprawled out in the mud. Not a perfect throw by any means but Louie reaches out and catches it easily just as the clap of thunder from that lightning rumbles through and just as the runner from third barrels into home and just as Coach Manton's obscenity-filled outburst flies from the dugout. The grand collision of ball and players and weather and cheering parents and screaming coach...stops.

A moment suspended in time as we all wait to hear the umpire's call.

And wait.

"Ouuuuuuut!" The ump jerks his thumb like a crazy hitchhiker.

I am just a few feet from the action, and I know in my bones that the kid was safe. He jumps up, furious, knowing the same thing. His coach complains. There are enthusiastic boos coming from that side of the stands. Now that the other coach is losing it, Coach

Manton is calm. He's the picture of restraint all the sudden.

Just then, the ump calls the game on account of lightning.

We win.

Fifth place. Yay.

As we are packing up our equipment bags, the sun peeks out and turns the world into a sauna. Coach yells at us for awhile, then we head toward the parking lot.

"Let's go to the pool!" Butch is always ready to extend the fun.

5

"The pool sounds good," says Louie. "Real good."

"Simmons? You in?" Butch says.

"Uh, I'm not sure...I gotta see..."

Nothing would feel better on this hot humid afternoon than getting out of this muddy catcher's gear and diving into that cool water, but I always get nervous about going to Cedar Hills Athletic Club. There is a little desk at the front where, hypothetically, they are supposed to make sure you are a neighborhood member. In reality, I have never seen anyone at that little desk ever, and I have been to the pool tons, dozens and dozens of times, over the years. But you see, I'm not a member. Our duplex is one street over from where the actual border of the Cedar Hills neighborhood ends – I know because I looked it up on the club's website. Probably nobody else knows or cares about official membership, I mean the "club" is just a swimming pool with a basketball hoop behind it and two tennis courts that probably need to be resurfaced. Still, there is a weathered "Members Only" sign on the gate that always gives me sweaty palms as I walk up.

"Pete, you wanna ride with me?" asks Richard, in his usual soft-spoken way.

"Well, I should shower and stuff – get my bathing suit."

"I've got extra. Just come with us," Richard says. He kind of shrugs as he waits for my answer. If I didn't know who he was, I'd say he was shy sometimes.

The real reason Richard probably wants me to go is so he won't be alone in the car with Mr. Loezier. Although Richard did make an amazing catch at third today, where he snagged a screaming line drive. It all happened so fast it seemed like a superhuman feat or something. Still, Mr. Loezier will no doubt find something to complain about.

"Yeah, sure, okay thanks. Lemme just tell my dad I'm going with you."

The Loeziers' old house was recently bought by Tommy Lee Jones. You know, that actor guy. Apparently Jones just like, knocked on the door and said he wanted it. Or maybe he came to a party there and made them a huge offer or something like that. There are a lot of stories. Anyway, the Loeziers built themselves a new, even better house up on one of those really high hills west of Austin. There's a view of forever up there. Aren't you glad you know the whole history of their housing situation now?

The point is, Richard's room has this whole wall of shelves with what must be every single trophy he ever got for anything. He had these shelves in his old house too, and then they moved them all here and set up every single trophy. His mom told me that Richard "just has to have them" but I think he actually hates having all those awards and medals stare at him every night. Half of them are from, like, elementary school soccer and stuff like that.

It's weird, but the most excited I ever saw Richard get was last summer when he told me about this computer camp he went to, where they designed their own iPhone apps and stuff. I didn't understand half of what he was saying, but it must've been kind of cool. He even signed up for a summer school class about it, but he wound up having to quit halfway through because we had a make-up tournament. He said he was glad though, because the class was actually a lot of work.

The bathing suit I borrow is a little small but it is still nicer than mine. It's one of those really cool surfer brands. I ask where he got it and Richard says maybe on vacation at Aruba or somewhere. He can't remember exactly, but on one of their trips. My swimsuit is something my mom got at Target – I used to really like it, but it's not anything like this one. Who knew swim trunks could be fancy?

Butch and Louie are already doing cannonballs off the diving board when we get there. Of course Richard and I breeze right in and there's no one at that little desk by the gate. Like I said, there never is. My first dive into that pool feels so frickin' good that I just stay under as long as my lungs can take it. The turquoise world of water, all quiet and weightless. It's the opposite of the pressure that was dragging me down on the stormy ball field this afternoon.

We all horse around and have races and

dunk each other and try to spit pool water the furthest. Butch finds some kind of little underwater dart bomb, and we throw it at each other in some made up version of tag. There's nothing like a game that is just created on the spot – those are the best. Louie keeps changing the rules every time Richard pegs him, but none of us really care. Butch says he better stop or "that's it," in his best Manton impersonation. It's pretty funny.

We finally get out and none of us have towels but we just lie directly on the poolside and soak up the warmth of the tiles there. I start thinking about today's baseball games and every last little error and all the ways we could've maybe changed things in that last game. And Coach Manton's face. And that weird old man staring at me as I walked from third back to the dugout.

"I didn't know they let you guys in here."

I open my eyes with a start. The shadow of Livvie falls over my face and I can see the sun coming through the blond curls around her face.

"Well, you have to know the right people," Butch says.

"So...fifth place." Livvie puts her foot on

her brother, like she might push him in. "That sucks."

"You should know," he says.

"Hey, we won first!" Livvie says. She holds up the Centex Volleyball Champions medal that's hanging around her neck.

Louie grabs her leg and swings her over him and splash! Right into the pool.

Livvie splutters to the surface. "You jerk!"

The guys are all laughing.

"My medal came off," Livvie says.

I think I spot it on the bottom of the pool and I dive in, going deep for it. I have to get a breath and go down a couple more times before I can snag the medal because it's kind of stuck in the drain cover. By the time I get it, the guys have gone over to shoot baskets and Livvie is sitting alone on the side of the pool.

"Thanks, Pete."

She reaches for my hand that's holding the medal, and wraps her hand around mine. And holds on.

"You're welcome."

She smiles, that Livvie smile I love. For a second, it's sort of the only thing that matters in this whole world. Just hanging out here with Livvie.

"Did you see the ads for that new Will Ferrell movie?" she asks.

"Oh yeah, he works at that nuclear bomb place –"

"And accidentally starts the countdown –"

"With that guy from *Stepbrothers* as the foreign guy –"

"John C. Reilly, he's hilarious!"

Our discussion of upcoming summer movies is eventually interrupted by a chant of "Get Livvie! Get Livvie!" Her volleyball teammates have arrived in force and they promptly push her in the pool.

"What is it with everyone throwing me in today?" Livvie laughs as she treads water and taps the side of her head to empty her ear.

Then all the guys and the girls swim a bit and Butch uses the underwater dart to try and hit the girls in all the wrong places. Louie is cracking up about it but I pretend not to notice. Richard gets stuck talking to some old man in a lounge chair who is asking a lot of boring questions about the jewelry stores. Soon my mom drives up. I hurry to leave, not because I really want to go but because I would prefer that our Prius, with all its crazy bumperstickers for various save-the-world causes, be parked out front for as short a time as possible. Besides, you never know when Mom is going to start up a conversation and tell people how they should xeriscape their yards instead of having sprinklers water their beautiful green grass, or how they should purchase carbon offsets to make up for their trip to the Bahamas. What does "carbon offsets" even mean? Don't ask me. And please don't ask her.

I scoop up my stuff and jog toward the exit, giving Richard a goodbye nod. He asks me to sleep over but I tell him I want to get some rest before practice tomorrow.

I know, I know... I'm lame, what can I say? But I learned my lesson after that xBox marathon last night.

Livvie intercepts me right at the gate.

"Hi, Mrs. Simmons!" She and my mom always have to make a big smiley greeting to each other. For some reason, I wish they wouldn't be so friendly.

"Hello, Olivia! How's your summer so far?"

"Well, first place this weekend." Livvie is

wearing her medal again, a little damp but still shiny, over her bathing suit.

"You go, girl!" Why does my mother have to say things like 'you go, girl' instead of just congratulations?

Livvie grabs my arm. "Hey, text me later."

"Okay." The way I say okay, you might think she was asking me to do her homework for her.

And then the weirdest thing happens. Livvie reaches up and kisses me on the cheek. On the one hand, it feels like the most normal thing in the world. It was just a natural extension of how Livvie is always friendly with everybody and on top of that, she and I are pretty good friends – almost like brother and sister in a way, so it was just a regular thing to do. On the other hand, Livvie has just kissed me – on the cheek but still kissed me – right in front of my mother. If Mom wasn't there I might react differently, but I am kind of like, shocked.

I freeze for one second. Actually for a couple of seconds – my whole body stops in its tracks while I am trying to process this kiss in my mind. What just happened? What did it mean? What should I do?

And why does this have to be happening in front of my mother?

"Sorry," whispers Livvie. And she turns and runs, all the way to the pool, and dives deep, out of sight.

6

P ractice starts out like any other: long toss, fielding, game situations. But this practice isn't like any other because we've been losing lately. Two weekends in a row. "Slump" is not in Manton's vocabulary, as far as I know. There are no natural ups and downs, as far as he's concerned. He expects us to win, win, win and get better, better, better. And for the last three years, we have.

Until now.

In the middle of one of the manufactured game situations (bases loaded, 3-2 count), I am crouched behind the plate catching Flat-

Top. Flat-Top got his name because he has kind of long hair, at least long by Coach Manton's standards, so Coach would always say he's going to hold him down and shave his head and give him a flat-top. Flat-Top just laughs and is mellow about it. He's one of those guys who never gets too upset about anything.

Which is good, because Flat-Top is not exactly a hot pitcher. I mean, sometimes it's like he doesn't even care that much, it's all just fun-and-games for him. He's a middle reliever that Manton uses when we are ahead by a lot. I've heard guys on the team say that Flat-Top's grandfather arranges fields from the city for Coach Manton to use for practice and that's the reason Flat-Top gets any time at all on the mound. To tell you the truth, I don't buy that. Coach Manton wants to win too badly to go for that. Besides, Flat-Top's got power, no doubt – he just hasn't mastered his control quite yet. Flat-Top is an investment in the future – if he tries, one day he will do big things, probably even more than Louie. I'll bet Flat-Top might be a starter by the time we're all on varsity.

Knock wood.

Anyway, Flat-Top's wild pitches have me reaching for the stars every time. Jump up three feet, lunge to the left, dig it out of the dirt. Every pitch is an adventure today. And he throws so hard, my thumb's beginning to hurt. I'll have to ice it again tonight.

During practices, I get to call the pitches. I signal low and outside and Flat-Top throws a knuckleball, high. I think I know why they call them knuckleballs. Anyway, it gets by me.

"Goddamn it, Simmons!" Manton roars as he walks toward me with purpose. "I am sick of this team having to carry you!"

"Yessir!" I grit my teeth. Carry me? I was Most Valuable Defensive Player of the Plano Junior Classic tourney just a couple of months ago. And that's not MVP of my team, but MVP of the whole tournament. And it was a big tourney, twenty-four teams.

I can't think that way! No one player is more important than all the others.

I repeat, "Yessir!" with more enthusiasm.

"If it were left up to you, we would've lost that game last night!" he shouts. "That passed ball and wimpy little throw to Louie was pathetic!"

I don't react, but I'm thinking – they called the guy out,   Coach. But I'm also thinking – he's right, the guy really was safe.

"I'll get somebody behind the plate who can keep the balls in front of him, goddammit!" He spits on the ground and it lands about four inches from my foot.

"If you wanna be a part of this team, you better – "

I do not say a word, I just barely shift my weight from one foot to the other.

"WHAT WAS THAT?"

I do not mean to show any disrespect, but maybe he is reading my mind.

Coach Manton stares at me, fuming. "I will replace you so fast, your head will spin! Kind of like it was spinning last night!"

Everybody on the field watches Coach Manton now, as he does an impersonation of me. He twists back and forth and sings out in a falsetto, "Where's the ball? Where's the little ballie? The one I don't know how to catch?"

Flat-Top snickers on the mound. I don't hold it against him. It's one of those nervous laughs that come out when you're thinking, please don't let me be next.

"Oh, there's the ball!" Manton makes a limp-wristed little gallop toward me, accompanied by a high-pitched giggle.

My face is hot. I'm still in my squat and I keep my eyes on the ground. I know everyone's watching, but there's no way to escape. No choice but to take it.

Manton is next to me now. He reaches down to get the ball out of my glove. I hold open my mitt so he can grab the baseball, but when he gets real close – I don't know if it's an accident and he just stumbles or loses his balance or something – wait, scratch that. What am I saying? I do know. I'm certain. What is happening is not an accident.

He knees me right in the chest. Even with my catcher's gear on, it hurts like hell. Right in the old sternum, it knocks the wind out of me and sends me flying back. I land on my butt, caught in that scary sensation of not being able to breathe. Nothing matters in that moment but getting air.

"Lose your balance, Simmons?" Manton is back to using his regular voice. "Bellows, get your gear on and get out here!"

Jeff Bellows, wide-eyed, looks from me to Coach. Most everyone else does the same thing. I see Butch's mouth hanging wide open.

"Bellows! Now!"

Bellows buckles up his shin guards as quickly as he can. I am finally getting a little oxygen, but not nearly enough. I stagger to my feet and lurch toward the dugout, gasping.

I get a couple of full lungs of air and the panic slightly subsides. I slump on the bench, trying to regain my composure. No one comes to check on me, and I'm glad.

What just happened? What did I do?

What set off Coach? I must've been really sloppy out there. I've got to try harder.

The minutes slowly turn into an hour, and I am still sitting there.

It is weird being in the dugout watching practice like this, a new experience for me. I try not to think about what just happened, but my mind keeps going back over it. This is probably the worst blow-up I've ever witnessed from Manton. Definitely the worst one directed straight at me. But I know how they all end. Once Manton gets it out of his system, he comes around. Pretty soon he'll just point at me and I'll go back behind the plate and all will be forgotten. I wait, alert and ready, for my chance to go back on the field.

Bellows is doing a decent job back there right now, I have to admit. But Jeff always makes it clear that he prefers playing the outfield so I know he's not gunning for my position. Anyway, he is an awesome power hitter and that's his specialty. Catching or not, he'll always be an asset to any team.

Still, I'd be lying if I didn't admit I'm a little bit happy to see an easy curve ball get past Bellows. And then another one.

I sit patiently, waiting for Coach to point at me. When he finally does, I sprint to my position and finish out the practice, everything back to normal.

I guess.

7

My parents have some great ideas on how I can work this summer, said *no one ever.*

They discuss their "interesting leads" with me at dinner. They've decided that this summer I can either get a job (Dad smiles encouragingly at that idea) or I can do community service (nudge, nudge from Mom).

"Wow, that is an exciting choice." They pretend not to notice I'm being sarcastic.

I grab another ear of corn on the cob. I can eat, like, as many ears of corn as my mom makes. The butter drips down my chin as Mom talks about how great volunteering looks on your high school transcript.

My phone buzzes – Richard is asking me to come play hoops. His sport court is lighted, so we can go late. I reply: *Be there soon.*

"So, which one?" my mom says.

"Um, volunteering." I decide on the spot. Volunteering sounds like it would give me more flexibility for baseball. A real job might make me late to practice or something, which would be unacceptable.

Richard texts back: *Don't come till 9:30.*

"Are you sure you don't want to make money? They need baggers down at the grocery store," my dad says.

I don't take the hint.

"Unless you aren't paying for my baseball fees anymore, I don't really need money, Dad."

"He's got you there," my mom says. "You give him everything, so he doesn't have to work."

"His baseball is work! All those hours of practice."

My mom rolls her eyes. "Believe it or not, baseball is supposed to be fun."

Dad turns back to me. "Of course we're

paying for your baseball fees, Pete, but I was wondering...I mean, what about money to go out, have some fun?"

For some reason that really ticks me off, the idea that my dad is talking to me about going out. Is he hinting that I should go out with a girl? Obviously, I don't ever do that and I guess he thinks that I'm weird or something.

"Thanks for dinner," I tell Mom as I push my chair back.

"Oh well...you're welcome," Mom says.

"And um, volunteering, yeah. Sounds good. Also I'm going to Richard's later," I say as I head to my room.

Lying on my bed with my headphones on and my eyes closed, I can really think about things. And I guess it's not too surprising that my thoughts wind up on Livvie. For some reason, I think back to the first time I ever talked to her...not that it was incredibly amazing or anything, but it was...Livvie.

My first day of sixth grade at Welton Middle School was not that fun. Neither was my first week. And by "not fun," I actually mean "a living hell."

At my elemen-   tary school in East

Austin, I had been with basically all the same people since kindergarten, so it never really occurred to any of us to try and be popular or figure out who was friends with who or anything like that – we just all knew each other and that was that. There was one guy, Julio, and I guess he was a good friend of mine or whatever. I mean we would spend the night at each other's house occasionally and he was usually on my Little League team and stuff like that, but we weren't soul-mate-brothers-for-life or anything. It was more like a relationship based on occasional wiffle ball marathons out in the street. Anyway I lost touch with him when I moved. It was just totally different back then. If somebody in elementary school had a birthday party or there was a school carnival or something, you would go or you wouldn't go, none of it ever seemed like a big deal. You hung out with whoever was around, just whatever. No big deal.

You could say things were a bit different when I got to Welton. Like a complete 360. Wait, I mean a 180. I always get those confused.

Anyway, at Welton I suddenly became aware of something called popularity. Maybe you've heard of it? Turns out I didn't have any. I'm not sure if I was unpopular because I was new and didn't know anyone, or if it would have been the same at the beginning of any middle school. Or maybe I was just one of those kids they talk about in that special "personal responsibility" unit in health class – you know: the kids who are entering their awkward puberty years and have no friends so they go home and cry into their pillow every night? JK on that last one. Even I am not that lame. I only cried every other night.

But seriously, I would've done about anything to make a friend. Walking around Welton was a whole new experience. For one thing, the halls were wide and the floors were shiny. And the people were blond and their teeth were shiny. It was weird because suddenly I didn't have one word to say to anybody. It was like I had entered an alternate universe, and in this one I was clueless and shy when anyone talked to me. Not that I ever had the opportunity to have a conversation, seeing as I was basically invisible.

All the other kids were so happy to run into their friends, like, "I haven't seen you *all summer*, how are you doing, you look *great*, how was Monserrat, how was Italy, how were the Galapagos, how was Napa, how was *Biar-*

ritz?" Lunch hour was like a geography lesson. I mean, was I really going to chime in about our long, hot trip in the Prius to see the Baseball Hall of Fame in Cooperstown? Followed by a stop at Niagara Falls, no less. And I'm not kidding, that was the farthest I'd ever been from home. It's still the farthest I've ever been from home actually. And by the way, Niagara Falls actually is amazing. But something tells me my new classmates at Welton Middle School would not have been impressed.

There are always people who complain about P.E., but it really isn't so bad at Welton. The gym has a rock climbing wall and the locker room has individual showers. Plus it is a class that does not require talking (which I did not want to do) but does require physical activity (which I really wanted to do). It quickly became the best part of the day. Toward the end of the first week, a flyer was posted on the bulletin board outside the locker room announcing a fall baseball team forming, the Texas Blaze. Tryouts on Friday after school. And that was when a tiny ray of hope entered my universe.

Fall ball.

I heard a couple of the real popular guys saying they were probably going to do it. You know, check it out, see if it was worth it. That was Louie and Butch talking. Funny how I thought of them then, as the cool guys. Now they are just my best friends. They are still really popular though.

Anyway, I figured what did I have to lose, so on Friday I stuffed my catcher's mitt in my backpack, down underneath the books so no one would see it at school. I told my dad to pick me up later than usual and when the final bell rang, I meandered over towards the field. I figured if I just strolled over casually, I could always back out at any moment.

There were about 45 guys on the field, most of them in baseball pants and cleats. No way I was going to join that group and look like a fool in my shorts and sneakers. Why hadn't I realized you were supposed to wear baseball pants? Stupid! At least I'd worn a baseball cap, but why did it have to say Garrido Little League? How lame was that? So I figured I'd just loop around the field like that was my normal path on the way to meet my dad. That way I'd get a look at the other guys and how well they could play. Just out of curiosity, you know.

And how well could they play? *Really* well, it turns out. I was getting more intimidated by the minute, seeing some of these guys zip the ball around the infield with precision. It was hypnotic, each throw so perfect.

"Heads up!" somebody shouted.

I looked up just in time to see a ball screaming towards me. I guess I could've ducked, but on instinct I whipped the cap off my head and caught the ball in it. I heard a couple of hoots and laughs from the field. I was ready to turn and run, but first I had to get the ball back to them.

"Right here!" Butch was about 100 feet away from me, motioning for the ball.

A couple of other guys were laughing. I just wanted to get rid of the ball and get out of there. I threw it to Butch, as hard as I could. The throw was right on the money. I turned and speed-walked towards the parking lot.

"Hey! Kid! Stop! I said STOP!"

And that was the first time Coach Manton yelled at me. Cool memory, in a way. I mean, you have to know Coach to fully appreciate that yelling is how he shows his...his everything.

So Coach brought me on the field, and even though I was kind of, like, mortified at the idea of being on the field in my shorts, I didn't have a lot of time to think about it. Coach Manton indoctrinated all of us that day into the very fast-paced practices he likes to run. We went from drill to drill, being timed and tested and measured for two hours. My dad and a lot of other parents were parked and watching for a long time before it was over.

Coach Manton let the players leave, one by one. By the time I realized what was happening, there were fourteen boys left and I was one of them.

"Bring it in!" he commanded.

We quickly huddled around him, eager to please.

"Anyone who is still here is being offered a position on my Texas Blaze 12U team. Think long and hard about whether you want to be on this team. It is going to be a very, very good team."

You could've heard a baseball drop in the outfield. We were all motionless. And suppressing smiles.

"And how do I know that we are going to be a very, very good team? Well for one thing, I am looking at some very special talent sitting in front of me right now. And you are a lucky team, because you have an excellent coach."

A couple of guys smiled, but Coach Manton did not appear to be kidding.

"And let's be clear on this, I am the one and only coach here. In all my years of doing this, I've never had an assistant. Don't need one, don't want one."

He stared long and hard, as if one of us kids was going to jump up and demand to have an assistant coach or something.

"Another reason I know this will be a good team is because we are going to work harder than any other team out there. And let me tell you, those other teams work extremely hard. But we are going to work just that much harder, to ensure our success. Now think very carefully about whether you have what it takes to be on the Texas Blaze. About how hard you are willing to work."

By this time, I was practically salivating, ready to give up anything for the opportunity to play for Coach Manton. To be on the Texas Blaze. To be part of something.

"We will practice three times a week and have tournaments at least every other weekend. If you have a girlfriend –"

There were some giggles. Most of us were still eleven and the girlfriend concept had not really solidified for us yet.

"HEY!" Coach Manton's voice was shockingly loud.

The team went silent. He took his time, then began talking again.

"—if you have a girlfriend, you will never get to see her. If you play another sport, you will have to give it up. If you are in choir or a church group or FFA or Boy Scouts, that will have to come second. A very distant second. As in, you should probably just quit it now. If you are late for practice, I mean if you are even one minute late for any practice ever, you will be benched. If you do not work hard, you will be benched. If you are disrespectful, you will be benched. If you are out of uniform, you will be benched. If you are always on time and you work your absolute hardest and you are respectful and you are in uniform...you still might be benched."

I remember I saw Louie kind of roll his eyes at Butch and Butch tried not to laugh. Coach didn't see them though. The threats and conditions and warnings went on for about half an hour, but it didn't matter. All of us were still willing to sign on the dotted line by the end. Coach Manton finally called the parents over and gave them the kinder, gentler version of his spiel which basically talked about what incredibly talented sons they all had and how they could pay by the month or for the whole semester in advance. Oh yeah, and not to plan any weekends out of town without checking with him first.

Life at Welton Middle School slowly started to change for me. Not only did I have something to do and somewhere to go, but I had somebody to be. The days I wore my Texas Blaze t-shirt, I even blended in with the other kids. And I began to get to know my teammates. Louie called me Asian Boy, even though I am not Asian and it does not rhyme with my name or anything. I was never 100% sure how it got started? Maybe something to do with East Austin and how Asian countries are also in the East? Honestly, I'm not sure I ever really understood why he called me that, but somehow it caught on and lasted for a few months. Yeah, maybe it was a racial slur and maybe it was the most decidedly un-catchy name ever, but no matter – I was secretly kind of thrilled every time I passed Louie in the hallway and he would shout,

"Hey Asian Boy!" I would laugh and wave and say, "Hey Louie!" It felt good to finally fit in.

"Why do you let him call you that?" One day, Livvie came up to my locker.

I had never talked to her before but we had Language Arts together so I knew who she was. And I knew she wasn't usually this angry.

"Uh...I..."

"That's a horrible nickname. It's an insult to Asian people! And that's the way he means it, don't you know that?"

"Louie's a good guy," I said.

"No, he's not. He's insulting you, or at least trying to. He's a jerk!"

I couldn't let this girl get away with insulting my teammates.

"He's not a jerk," I told her. And I shut my locker with some force.

I stood my ground. I knew that being loyal to this team was my only chance for survival at Welton, and I wasn't about to let this girl insult my new friends. My only friends.

"Okay, okay, relax." She seemed surprised and gave me a good once-over, ending in a smile. "Louie's my brother, you know. We're twins."

All the sudden, I could see it in her face. A few freckles sprinkled across the nose, those dirty blond curls, the ready smile. Louie and Livvie were definitely related.

"But trust me, he *is* a jerk," she said. With a big grin, she punched me in the shoulder and kept on walking. "By the way, I'm Livvie. Nice to meet you, Pete."

8

Richard's sport court has speakers with loud music and those really cool glass basketball goals and a soft springy surface that doesn't make your ankles hurt and an ivy-covered fence all the way around it. Louie adjusts one of the hoops to eight feet so we can dunk on it. Honestly, I know that's sort of a pointless thing to do, but it's fun as hell. We take turns going all LeBron, slamming the leather ball through the hoop. Butch can barely jump but he's already so tall that he mostly dominates. I try a reverse double pump, something I've seen Blake Griffin do on TV. I almost gct it, but almost really does not count when it comes to dunking a basketball. I sort of bang up my wrist but pretend it doesn't hurt.

Eventually we are in the kitchen where Richard's housekeeper has left trays of cookies and snacks. The Loeziers are out at some "charity function," as Richard puts it. The housekeeper pretty much sticks to her room off the kitchen, but she keeps her door open and I can hear a TV show in Spanish going in there.

"Where's the liquor cabinet around here?" asks Butch.

"Can I toast a bagel?" asks Bellows.

"Sure, bagels right over there," says Richard. "And there's cream cheese in that little fridge."

Richard's always a gracious host and knows the right thing to say – I think it's been practically drilled into him. He actually went to manners classes called Cotillion. Most of the guys around here went, but my folks never sent me. They have it every spring at the country club and you have to wear a jacket and tie and learn ballroom dancing and which fork to use. Everybody was always like, "You are SOOOO lucky you don't have to go!" My parents are cool that way. But I sometimes wonder if I missed learning that double secret special handshake that the rest of the guys all use to let them into the polite club. I might be doing something rude on accident all the time, who knows.

"Seriously, where's the liquor cabinet?" Butch is poking around, opening things and actively looking for alcohol.

"Come on, guys...let's see what's on the MLB channel." Richard attempts to lead us into the TV room.

Butch finds the motherlode: dozens of bottles of amber liquids with shiny metallic labels. "That's what I'm talking about!"

I see Richard glance toward the maid's room. She may not say much, but I know she can hear us. And I know she might tell Mr. Loezier what's going on. And I know that drinking any of that liquor is about as smart as standing in the middle of I-35 at rush hour. But who is going to admit that?

Richard looks pretty nervous.

"Did you guys hear Alicia Caldwell started her own YouTube channel?" I blurt out.

I'm not sure how I came up with that subject, but I am just trying to get everybody's attention. Alicia is the most glamorous girl in Welton Heights and I know every guy would be at least slightly interested in watching videos of her.

Butch slams the cabinet door shut. "Where's your laptop, Richard?"

Alicia's videos wind up being about how to put on mascara and the best way to use a curling iron, but we still watch a few of them. It's fun to make jokes about them, but it's also fun to see Alicia sitting on her all-pink bed in her all-pink room with her tiny fluffy dog in her lap. Louie posts a supposedly anonymous comment on Alicia's YouTube channel that says, "Can you do a video about bikini waxing?"

Guys are cracking up but Richard says, "This won't be traced to my computer or anything, will it?"

Then Louie starts accusing Richard of having a crush on Alicia and jokes around saying, "Stick to the girls at St. Anthony's!"

By the time the guys are finally watching a Giants vs Dodgers game (and mostly hating on both teams the whole time), I am trying to straighten up the kitchen a little. Two words for you: Cracker Fight. There are crumbs everywhere.

"You really don't have to do that," says

Richard.

"Well, I don't want your mom freaking out," I tell him.

"That's not likely. She's in Santa Fe."

"Oh yeah?"

"A yoga retreat..."

"Cool."

I'm sweeping up. Richard is staring off into space.

"Yeah," he says. "She really likes it. Apparently... Yoga, I mean."

We hear the hum of the electric garage door. Mr. Loezier must be home. Richard jumps up and starts helping me brush away the crumbs.

Butch comes in, holding the Loeziers' phone, with his hand over the mouthpiece.

"It's Alicia Caldwell! We just called her and she wants to talk to you!" Butch shoves the phone at Richard.

"What? Who called her?" Richard lets a bit of slight irritation show through his usual implacable demeanor.

I take the phone and tell her I'm sorry for my stupid friends and Richard's busy. Richard smiles and gives me a silent nod of thanks.

9

Another day. Another practice. Another time I am sitting on the bench. I try to push down the part of me that's panicking: *Why did Coach put in Bellows again? Did I do something wrong? What am I doing on the bench?* And instead I try to think rationally: *Every team has to have at least two catchers. Watch and learn. Try to relax. He's going to call you out there any minute.*

I am so busy making a mental inventory of every pitch that Bellows is catching and how he frames it up, that I miss what exactly starts it all. I just see Louie heading straight toward where I am in the dugout, with Coach

Manton not far behind.

"If you don't know by now that you are supposed to *get behind* a ground ball instead of sticking your glove out, then you don't know the first thing about baseball. Hopeless! You hear me? That's what you are!"

Louie's face is red, but not because of the summer temperature.

"Me catch it!" Manton starts an impersonation of Louie now, using a stupid caveman voice. He sticks his pretend glove way out to the side. "Ball no go! Me mad!"

Louie drops his mitt on the bench and plunks down a few feet from me.

"What's wrong, Louie? Why don't you call your dad and tell him coach was mean to you?" Manton laughs and turns to walk away.

Louie whispers, "Frickin' jerk."

My head snaps up as quickly as Manton spins around. Louie stares straight ahead. I try to play it cool.

"Burns! You got something to say to me?!"

"No sir," says Louie.

Manton comes closer, right outside the dugout now, looking at us through the fence.

Players are gathering, inching closer.

"WHAT DID YOU SAY?!"

"No sir!" Louie manages.

"How about you, Simmons?" Manton turns into his most menacing self, an insane gleam in his eye. It is like someone else inhabits his body here lately. Losing games these past few weekends definitely has not agreed with him.

I try not to make eye contact. "No sir!"

A moment of silence. Stillness...Manton stares at the two of us, back and forth.

And Louie takes a deep breath and lets out a sigh. I honestly think he is just trying to get some oxygen, but it must come across as disrespectful to Coach Manton.

"Why you little—"

Manton runs toward Louie. And I mean RUNS, full speed, around the fence and into the dugout. Can I just say, Manton is not a small man. His eyes are wild, I can feel the adrenaline vibrating through every part of his fight-or-flight brain.

"YOU GOT SOMETHING TO SAY TO ME, BURNS?"

He grabs the front of Louie's shirt and lifts him up on his toes. I swear, little bubbles of spit are at the corner of Manton's lips. He is literally frothing at the mouth.

"SAY IT TO MY FACE!"

"Okay, okay!" I hear Louie say as Manton shakes him.

I think he's saying "okay, okay" please let me go, not "okay, okay" I'll say it to your face. But Manton is enraged even further.

Even the outfielders are jogging toward us now. I think maybe everybody is getting ready to save Louie's life or something. And I wonder if they might be too late. Manton sort of bangs Louie into the wall of the dugout. I see Louie's head hit the wood and sort of jerk back. He's like limp spaghetti in Coach Manton's grip.

"STOP!" I kind of push myself between the two of them, holding Manton away with two hands to his chest. "Get away from him!"

After approximately two of the longest seconds of my life, Manton lets go and Louie lands on the bench.

I try and get ready to face Manton, no matter what comes next. All the players are nearby now, witnessing this. They've got my back.

And Manton smiles. Pure pleasure comes over his face. Somehow, this is the scariest thing of all.

"Okay," he purrs. "Go ahead. What are you going to do?"

He keeps smiling at me for a long time, or at least it feels like a long time. My heart is pounding like the hip hop bass in a teenager's car. I feel like everyone can hear it.

Finally, as if he's shooing a mosquito, Coach Manton sweeps his arm around and knocks me to the ground. As I go down, I hit my side and then my head on the bench. A sharp pain zips through my rib cage.

I am on the ground staring at Manton's perfectly clean Nikes. I glance up to see Louie's wide eyes. I try to breathe normally, but I am strangely dizzy and sleepy all the sudden. I think my brain just wants to shut down and give up. Manton's leering grin seems to waver and blur in front of my face, in and out of focus.

For some reason I start flashing on all these weird memories: on playing catch with Richard a long time ago, on my mom's face when she's cooking dinner, on watching *The Simpsons* with my sister a long time ago, on sitting in Language Arts class behind Livvie while she twirls her hair around her finger. Just normal, regular things. And what would all those people think right now? Because this isn't normal, is it? Coach is going too far – everybody sees that.

Right?

Don't they?

"Come on, Simmons," Manton begs. "What are you going to do now?"

This is crazy.

"I quit," I whisper. I meant to say it differently, louder, but don't have enough air. What does it matter how I say it? I quit. I *have* to quit. We all do. That is the one thing that is actually clear in this moment. I mean, we can't take any more of this insanity. I'm sorry we've been losing games lately, but this is crazy. I pull myself back up to a standing position.

"I quit." This time it comes out a little more like my normal voice.

My eyes start to, like, water.

Coach stares at me for a long minute. Expressionless. A tear threatens to roll down my face. To cover it, I reach for my catcher's mask but Coach Manton knocks it out of my hands.

"Goodbye," says Coach Manton. He is the picture of calm – collected and cool all the sudden.

No one moves.

"I said goodbye. Now go," he nods toward the bags. "Pack up and leave."

I start to gather my stuff, staggering a little. Everyone watches me. It's hard to stuff everything in. I can't zip up my bag.

"And Pete, tell your parents no refunds. I know they need the money, but we aren't running a charity here."

I guess he really does know how to get to me. I feel a tear fall down my cheek as Coach Manton walks out of the dugout. He points players into different field positions and practice continues, as if everything is completely normal. Butch comes in and gives me a quick pat on the shoulder as he runs to center field.

"And Louie! You're at short, pal," Manton says matter-of-factly.

Louie never looks at me. He picks up his glove and runs out on the field.

I drag my bag out of the ballpark and

across the parking lot and down the street. The scrape-scrape of my metal cleats on the pavement is all I let myself think about, I just concentrate on how that sound makes my teeth hurt. That horrible noise keeps me from crying somehow.

I get about a half mile away before I even bother to take off my cleats and put on sneakers. When I finally pull out my cell phone, I just text my dad: *Can u pick me up in front of Walgreens?*

Then I stand alone on the side of the road, waiting.

10

I kind of, like, get all mad in the car on the way home and I pour out the whole story to my dad. Well, most of the story.

Well, some of the story.

I had been planning to just give Dad the silent treatment and say I didn't feel like talking, but he knows something is wrong. And then I sort of break down... I tell Dad about the yelling and about Louie getting in trouble and everything, but I don't exactly mention that Coach grabbed Louie's shirt or that he pushed me down. Not that Dad would freak out exactly, I mean he knows Coach gets pretty angry and loud at times. Everybody knows that. And it's not like Coach hit us, exactly. But I sort of leave that part out anyway.

It's not like I think Dad would go all crazy and want to call the head of the league or the authorities or whoever, to lodge a complaint. But my mom always tends to, like, *report* things. Call your representative. Write a letter. Make the world a better place. Blah, blah, blah. Good luck with that.

For now, I just don't feel like getting into it and it's just better to say I quit because Coach was yelling at us. I mean, that is true. Even if it's not the whole truth.

My dad pats me on the shoulder and tells me that my baseball career is a long journey and this is just a hiccup that I'll barely remember in the long run. He thinks I made a smart decision. Next year is high school and all of this select ball nonsense will be a distant memory. Tournament baseball is not real baseball anyway, according to him. There should never be time limits on a baseball game... He starts explaining his point of view on that subject, which I've heard a thousand times before.

Next spring, I'll be playing with my friends, proudly wearing school colors, maybe there will even be a pep rally or something. And in high school, baseball is a class you take, can you believe that? I'm already signed up for it, and we will do off-season workouts and fall ball before we even start the regular season in the spring. And sometimes freshmen even get moved up to JV. Or varsity. I actually met the high school coach at a day camp last summer, and he seems decent. Coach Smith. I know, right? Smith. And he seems like a Coach Smith. Plain. Vanilla. Quiet. Sounds good, doesn't it? Ha. Apparently he's been coaching for about 100 years. Nothing rattles him. What a change that will be.

The weird thing about crying is that it starts and stops when you least expect it.

Who am I kidding? How am I going to make the high school team, much less the *varsity*, if I've got this quitter's reputation? Coach Manton is going to tell Coach Smith terrible things about me – things that are true, I guess. I did quit, didn't I? And there is no place for quitters on the high school team.

I can't think like this.

That night my mom makes me mac 'n cheese from a box, even though it probably has seventeen different chemicals in it or whatever. She knows I've always liked it. My dad and I watch a really exciting basketball game. Oklahoma Thunder and Miami Heat, three overtimes. We have no connection to either team, but it is a great match up and there are some amazing dunks. Unbelievable that one of the guys playing is just five years older than me.

I'd love to play sports in college someday. All through elementary school, I used to say I was going to play baseball for Stanford. That was before I realized just about everybody who's anybody in the United States wants to go to Stanford University and that includes the best of the best who play baseball too. So now I've sort of refined my expectations, and realize no matter how many straight-A report cards I get, there are a million other kids out there doing the same thing. Although my mom says I have a good chance at one of the top schools if I keep working, I honestly think I would just like to find some cool smaller university with D-1 baseball...maybe study journalism or something... I fall asleep on the couch imagining running into Livvie, except now we are both in college and she plays on the volleyball team and I play on the baseball team. Or wait, are we in high school? Either way, it is a good dream and I say something that makes her laugh.

The dream ends when my phone buzzes with a text from Louie: *WTF man???*

It takes me a minute to get back to reality and figure out the answer. But I don't have an answer. What does Louie mean? Is he upset with me? Or is he complaining about Manton? Yeah, of course.

So I text back, *I know he's crazy.*

Louie writes back, *He's not the only one dude.*

I'm not sure I know what that means. I'm not sure I want to know. The texts come in occasionally throughout the afternoon and night but I don't reply to any more of them. Butch. Jeff. Flat-Top. Richard. And of course Livvie. Fourteen texts from Livvie alone:

What happened????

Manton is a jerk!!!!!!!!!!

How r u???

Are u ok?

Pete, write back when you get this

Hope ur ok

Want to talk... Call me.

Pete HELLOOOOOOOOOOOO?

Pete?

Pete

Just say you are ok and alive

Ok this is my last text!

I mean it this time

Ok this time

And then she stops. I don't answer, but I re-read Livvie's texts over and over. I can actually hear her voice saying each one. It is kind of weird actually. Wait, I'm hearing voices? That can't be good.

By mid-afternoon the next day, my bed is extremely uncomfortable, but I don't get up. I don't even move, yet I don't sleep either. I am sort of punishing myself by lying very, very still. If that sounds crazy, okay maybe it is.

I stare at my closet, noticing how the sliding louvered doors on the right side hang lopsided. They always come off the tracks, even if you just barely touch them, and that's why I haven't opened the right side of my closet in a couple of years. Funny the things you can get used to. I don't even think about it whenever I slide open the left door and gingerly reach around to get my stuff.

I see that it's 2:47. Practice starts at 3, which means everyone is arriving at the field by now. Ten minutes early is on time, as far as Coach Manton is concerned. And practice ending 45 minutes late – or more – is par for the course. All the parents talk or read on their phones while they wait, because everyone knows that practice never ends on time. But I guess I don't have to worry about that anymore...

My life is over, isn't it? C'mon, admit it. I'm screwed. I've gone back to being the invisible transfer student. I'm no longer on the Texas Blaze. I'm no longer a catcher. I no longer play baseball! I...I don't really do anything.

My life stretches out in front of me, empty. What am I going to do all summer? Without baseball, what is there to do?

And the one thing that I absolutely don't want to think about, pops into my head again. Out of all the millions of things crowding my mind that I would rather not concentrate on, this one might be the worst.

How am I supposed to make the high school team next year?

After all, that's the big question looming. I

mean if I don't play this summer, what will Coach Smith think? And if I don't make the high school team, what am I going to do? Who am I going to be? I'm a baseball player!

No, I am a guy who talks back to his coach. Who quits the team. I never thought that would be me.

But how much can a guy put up with? I mean Coach Manton hit me, right? Or at least, pushed me down. Kind of punched me right in the chest! Or did he lose his balance and just kind of knock into me? He was practically frothing at the mouth like a crazy man at the time, I know that for sure. I remember some of his spit hitting me in the face as he was screaming. Of course, all the good coaches are tough. Am I just a wimp who can't take it?

A couple of days go by, and I can finally muster up the energy to play video games and watch some SportsCenter. Then I go back to bed.

My parents play along at first, pretending I have "a cold" and giving me my space. I flip through old comic books and take a lot of naps. Over and over, I read what Livvie signed in my yearbook: *Pete, You don't realize a lot of things – like how good you are at base-*

ball for instance. And that Welton is a lot better since you transferred here. And other things too. Love ya! –Livvie

I almost wished it said "love" instead of "love ya." Or maybe "love ya" was better – at least it was directed at me instead of just a generic "love." But the "ya" was so casual and off the cuff... What was I doing? Analyzing some dumb thing that Livvie scrawled in about one minute and probably gave absolutely no thought to. What a loser I am.

Maybe that's why I "don't realize a lot of things."

11

By the second week of summer, my parents take action. I have to go sit at the table and eat dinner with them. My dad isn't even allowed to read a book and my mom puts out cloth napkins. Help me.

Somewhere between buttering my roll and taking a bite of my chicken leg, I am ambushed.

"So Petey, we were thinking," begins my mom.

I know something good is coming. And by "good," I mean bad.

It's a two-prong attack. One, I am going to have to pull the trigger and actually do that community service. I'd sort of conveniently forgotten all about it.

Turns out in high school, you have to fulfill a hundred hours of community service just to graduate, so the 'rents have decided I should get a jump on it. My mom says it would be good for me to help others less fortunate and etc etc. I zone out a little. This is the kind of stuff she is always talking about and I have heard it all before. I think she sees this summer's turn of events as an opening and she's pouncing. The words "Habitat for Humanity" and "soup kitchen" float around the room.

I eat and nod, not putting up a fight. I've learned what putting up a fight gets you. Ha.

That's not funny.

Part two of the Pete-Simmons-Rehabilitation-Project is private coaching. Okaaaay, was not expecting that one. This will "give structure to my workouts" and keep me baseball ready for high school. This part of the plan has my dad's fingerprints all over it. I don't even ask who the trainer is, just take another dinner roll and tell them it sounds fine.

Private training has sort of an elite sound to it, and I've always envied it when one of my teammates said they just had a "session with a pitching instructor" or "one-on-one batting lessons." There are even catching experts out there – lots of them. But that is something our family does not do, or more like cannot do. Until now, apparently. I guess they are willing to spring for it, seeing as I am so blue. Hey, this depression thing might turn out okay.

Kidding.

So it turns out the private coaching session is not as fancy and exotic as I imagined. Dad drives us deep into East Austin, even further than where we used to live. Further than the library where my mom works. It is an area where windows are boarded up and the graffiti is the freshest paint in the neighborhood.

"This is it?"

That is not a rhetorical question. I truly think maybe my dad is lost. The field is nothing more than a drooping backstop. No outfield fence. Only the barest outlines of where the base paths should be.

"C'mon, Pete. Give it a chance. This guy's supposed to be good. Really good."

I feel ridiculous lifting my baseball bag

out of the trunk and dragging it across the un-mown grass. There are no bleachers, no scoreboard. I am basically standing in an abandoned vacant lot.

"Hey," a young voice calls out. A guy with short dreadlocks gets out of a broken down Nissan.

My dad is sitting in the car, absorbed in a biography of Martin Scorsese. Mr. Dreadlocks is approaching me.

"I'm waiting for someone!" I let him know. I don't want any trouble. "A coach!" I add, for emphasis.

Dreadlocks smiles. "That's me!"

"What?"

"I'm the coach, man."

He can't be more than 25 or 26 and he is wearing blue jeans and flip-flops. I see that his tshirt reads: *Save the Planet – It's the only one with baseball.*

I take a step backward.

"Oh sorry, I think I..." What? What do I think I am doing?

"Pete Simmons? Catcher? Throws right, bats left?" His smile turns to a laugh. "Hi, I'm Ash."

We shake hands. My dad finally looks up. He and Ash wave at each other.

What is happening? This is not real baseball. My parents and their crazy ideas. This guy Ash is probably some hard luck story and my folks think it will be great to give him some work experience. I really don't feel like being coached by some weirdo just out of rehab or something. When I was about five, my babysitter was a convicted anti-government protester who was trying to get her life together. And so what do my parents do? Hire her to take care of me! Okay, so she was actually a grad student in molecular biology who had picketed a company that did animal testing...but she really had gone to jail for it.

"You have an extra glove?" Ash nods toward my huge rolling equipment bag. "Looks like there's room in there for quite a few gloves."

"Well, I have to carry my catcher's gear..." I know I sound defensive but I don't actually care.

"Of course, of course..." he smiles and squats by my bag. "Let's take a look."

He wants to look in my bag? I kneel down and unzip it, start digging through. It may look like a mess, but I know where everything is.

"Uh, I have an outfield glove, a first baseman's glove and my catcher's mitt..." I pull them out one by one.

"And what's this?" He plucks out that kids meal toy – the frog with the suction cup bottom. The one Livvie gave me at Whataburger that time.

"Uh, just trash." I grab it and throw it back in the bag.

He smiles and nods and takes the outfield glove. "Let's play catch."

Soft toss becomes long toss. No words are exchanged, no advice given, nothing is going on. I hope my dad isn't paying too much for this. Ash's throwing motion is one of those loose and easy things – looks like he's moving in slow motion but it's actually deceptively quick.

Finally Ash says, "Now, gun it to second as fast as you can."

I throw it to him at "second base," which is just a clump of weeds.

"Like you mean it," he says.

So I get into catcher's position and he

throws me the ball. I pop up immediately and throw it back with precision. I do it just the way I've been taught by Manton for years: low and to the right, so the short stop or second baseman will have their glove in position to make the tag as soon as they catch the ball. No matter that I am in the middle of an abandoned city park with none of my friends, it still feels good to make that throw. It feels right.

"Again," he says.

We do it a few more times, and on the last throw I am off a little and the ball almost gets past him. But Ash lays out and makes the stop. I can't help thinking that I've never seen a coach who could make a diving catch, much less jump right back up like one of the players.

"Okay, that's good." Ash tosses the out-fielder's glove to me as he walks toward the car.

He leans in the window and chats with my dad for several minutes, both of them laughing and gesturing. I take my time packing up.

You've gotta be kidding. That was a private coaching session? Playing catch?

115

My equipment bag now seems ostentatiously large as I roll it toward them. Hey, some of us actually need all this equipment, I think to myself. I put the bag in the back of the Prius and slam the hatch.

"Pete, come here a minute," my dad calls me. "Coach Keele has something to talk to you about."

"Coach Keele?"

"Yeah, I'm Ashland Keele. But you can call me Ash or Coach Keele, or just Key – that's what my friends call me."

"Yessir!"

Coach Keele and my dad exchange a look. Not sure what that means, but I just stand waiting.

"So Pete, your dad tells me you might be available, looking for a team."

"Uh-"

But Coach Keele doesn't let me talk. "Thing is, I'm putting together a team. Or trying to." He laughs, not afraid to admit he is unsure. "And you see, a catcher like you, well that would be just the thing to pull a team together. It would tip the scales, you know what I mean? Have you ever heard of that book, *The Tipping Point?*"

"Oh yeah, my wife read that," Dad interjects.

"Anyway, you just might be my tipping point," Coach tells me.

I think he can tell from looking at me that I have no idea what he's talking about. I am just ready to get out of this bizarre alternate universe and go watch an MLB game on TV.

"Uh, no sir. I can't." They are both looking at me expectantly. "I'm sorry. I'm kind of busy with...community service," I add.

My dad starts to say something but Ash puts his arm around me and walks me a couple of paces away. My dad takes the hint, starts the car and rolls up his window.

"Look, Pete, I'm not expecting an answer right now. Just think about it. And if the answer is no, that's cool. I completely understand where you're coming from."

Where I'm coming from? Gimme a break.

"Yessir!"

Coach Keele stops and stares at me for a few long seconds. "Coach Manton has taught you well."

I bristle at the sound of that. How much does this guy know about me?

"Yessir!"

"Yeah, I could recognize Manton's work anywhere. And I should be able to. I played for him myself, for two seasons. Two loooooong seasons." He laughs and waves, backing away. "Just think about it. No big deal. I have five guys so far. Billy D, the pitcher from Jefferson? You know him?"

Did I ever. Billy D struck out the side four innings in a row when we played them at a tourney in San Marcos last spring. I thought Coach Manton's head was going to explode. But we wound up winning anyway.

"Yeah, we got Billy D and a couple of others. Well, so, uh...your dad has my number."

He gets in his car and starts it. As he drives away, he turns his radio up. Loud. It is a good song. I see him bopping his head to the beat.

I get in the Prius.

"So, what community service did you decide on that's keeping you so busy?" my dad teases me.

"I'll find something."

12

That night, my friends descend on my house. I think Mom ran into Butch's mother at the grocery store and said the guys were welcome to come by after practice. Or something like that – she probably begged them to send their kids over. Who knows? I don't even want to know why they decide to visit the charity case (also known as me). Mom didn't tell me they might come, probably because she wasn't sure if they would show up or not – so I am in the middle of the 9th inning of this epic MLB 2K game and my mom yells up, like, "Petey, some friends have stopped by!"

It is immediately embarrassing when I

119

walk downstairs because Mom has actually straightened up the living room and made all these snacks that involve crackers and grapes and toothpicks and stuff. But my friends love it. They scarf basically every single thing that is set in front of them. Butch even eats one of the toothpicks, bit by bit. There is a Cardinals-Astros game on TV. Afterward, we go out to my driveway and shoot baskets even though my hoop is like the flimsiest, rustiest thing ever. The renters who lived here before left it out for the trash collectors, but my dad "fixed" it with – what else? – duct tape. Butch dunks on it and I think it will break, but the tape actually holds.

"You know, you're lucky," says Butch.

"How do you figure?" I ask him.

"Because Bellows is screwing up big time. Another day or two of this, and Coach M is going to be begging for you to come back."

"I'd doubt that." But I feel my stomach do a flip of excitement.

"Why? I mean, you didn't do anything wrong," Richard gives me a smile. It feels good to hear him say that. Maybe it's even true.

"Seriously, we all talked about it," Butch

is like a giant puppy when he gets excited. "Coach has to take you back! My dad's all like, 'without Simmons, we suck!'" Everybody laughs at Butch talking in a deep voice like his father. "And so my dad went and talked to Manton and was, like, 'we paid for this season and we want Simmons back!' So you're, like, in!"

Richard smiles. "It's true. Manton talked to my dad, too. He's taking you back. I mean, he said that you made a mistake but what do you expect of young boys and he was ready to forgive as long as you didn't let it happen again and all that... But listen, it's a miracle. He's going to let you back in!"

The guys all look at me expectantly. I realize they have been bursting with this good news since the moment they arrived, and had been waiting until we were alone outside. My buddies. They have my back. They are getting me back on the team again! That's the reason they came over, not because my mom said I was a pathetic lonely loser sitting home by myself.

It is all going to be okay. I laugh out loud.

We start a game of HORSE with my semi-flat basketball.

"So where's Louie tonight?" I ask.

Nobody looks at each other but they pause too long.

"I think he has something..." Flat-Top offers.

"Yeah," Butch agrees.

The silence becomes awkward.

"So coach really said that?" I ask them.

They all nod vigorously. I smile.

I am going to be back with my buddies! On the Texas Blaze, practicing every day, going to tournaments every weekend, back where I belong.

"It's unbelievable." I can't stop smiling.

"I know, right!" Butch punches me in the shoulder. "I thought no way, but he is going to give you another chance!"

"Oh yeah?"

Butch is on a roll. "Yeah! Manton was talking to Louie, and he said that Louie better set you straight, but Louie said... Well, anyway Coach is gonna forgive your mistake."

"You mean how I mistakenly got pushed down on the ground?"

"You know what I mean..." Butch realizes

he's maybe said too much.

"And what did Louie say?" I have to ask.

"Oh, you know Louie." Butch looks at Richard.

"So...is Louie going to set me straight?"

"Come on, Simmons!" Richard sees where I am going with this. He passes me the basketball.

"I mean, if he is, why isn't he here?" I shoot a free throw and it bounces off the rim.

Butch gets the rebound and throws the basketball back to me. "Hey, your mom got anymore of those crackers?"

"What did Louie say?" I ask again.

Richard is exasperated. "He just said you shouldn't let it happen again!" Richard shrugs. "And obviously, you shouldn't."

I hold the basketball in front of my face, like I'm getting ready to shoot. "You're right. I'm thinking I shouldn't let Manton hit me or push me around again. And the best way to do that is to not come back to the Texas Blaze."

"What's that supposed to mean?" Butch grabs the ball from me and bricks a three point shot.

"It means I've joined another team."

Richard is the first to start laughing. "Good one, Pete."

"I'm serious."

They stare as I explain that it's a new team just starting, with a young coach who was a short stop at Jefferson High School less than ten years ago. He took Jefferson all the way to the state championship and then went on to play at Dartmouth in the Ivy League for four years. And now this guy had come back to town recently to start this youth program.

You see, I googled Ashland Keele and have become quite the expert on his career now. Funny, while I was reading about him online I never dreamed I'd actually join the team. I thought I was just curious about him – looking him up for fun. But now that I say it out loud, I realize maybe I do want to play for Ash.

Why not?

"Seriously. I joined his team. He's cool."

"Cool??" To Butch and all the guys, this is a very weird way to describe a coach.

Right about then, Butch's dad pulls up in his gigantic SUV. The engine is super loud.

"I can't believe it..." Richard looks at me like I am a stranger. Or an enemy.

Butch's dad honks. "Let's go, boys!" Mr. Nikos is not somebody to keep waiting.

As the rest of the guys go to the car, Richard stands looking at me.

"What?" I try to smile. "I didn't do anything wrong, you said so yourself."

"That was before." Richard piles into the SUV.

"See you back on the field real soon!" Butch's dad waves at me. "And by the way, you're welcome!" He gives me a thumbs up.

I guess Butch or somebody tells Mr. Nikos right then and there that I have joined another team, because I hear him say "What the --??"

I let the screen door slam behind me as I go inside.

I finally respond to Livvie's texts. I write: *Guess what! I joined a new team.*

I fall asleep waiting for her to write back.

13

My mom hears about this "wonderful volunteer opportunity" from a flyer at the library. She says it sounds perfect for me since I am so passionate about my community service. She's always been hilarious.

Anyway, I guess it sort of does sound okay. It's basically being an assistant-assistant coach for a tee ball team. They play not far from where I'd met Ash the other day – on Cesar Chavez Field, my old stomping grounds back in kindergarten. Garrido Little League is always short-handed, according to my mom. They don't have too many dads with the free time to be involved, so they depend mostly on community volun-   teers. Like me. Yippee.

I know it isn't going to be the big show, but even my low expectations are undercut. At the first practice, all the boys wear cargo shorts and sandals and most of them don't have baseball gloves. Four boys bring bats, but they are all the wrong sizes, too heavy for them to swing and with big barrels that are illegal to use in Little League. One kid, Theo, wears a little plastic baseball glove that has Ninja Turtles printed on it.

"I like your glove," I tell him.

"I know." Theo nods in agreement. "It belongs to my big brother. I borrowed it." He is completely serious.

"That was nice of him, to let you use it."

"Yeah, he doesn't need it anymore. He used to play for Jefferson but he quit."

Playing for Jefferson is a big deal. Their team makes it to the playoffs on a regular basis.

"Oh, that's too bad. Why'd your brother quit baseball?"

"No, he quit school. Actually, he got spelled."

I'm thinking he means expelled.

I quickly learn not to ask too many personal questions because little kids will tell you a lot of stuff that their families probably don't want you to hear. Anyway, they all seem like regular, normal, okay kids and everything – but most have never even seen a baseball game much less played. So why are they here? I start to realize this baseball team is seen around the neighborhood as some free babysitting twice a week.

So we've got that going for us.

The two head coaches are Arnie and Zach. They are tall blond college guys, very earnest and enthusiastic. They have the boys say a prayer before practice and they cheer wildly if anyone actually gets a hit or catches a ball. Unfortunately, Arnie and Zach don't know much about baseball. They are thrilled to let me handle "that part of things." Kind of funny that they think baseball is just one small part of being a baseball coach...but by the time the first practice is half done, I realize they might be right. The bigger job is getting the boys to pay attention and stand still and wait their turn and not kill each other with the bats.

I am trying to show Theo how to hold a bat. He is not paying attention. I try again and again with no luck, until I finally get irritated. "Listen up!" I bark.

Theo's eyes get big. That tone of voice definitely gets his attention. And it's kind of funny – I sounded just like Coach Manton for a minute.

I kneel down next to Theo. "Sorry, buddy."

"That's okay," Theo says. He gives me a smile that says it really is okay, but I still feel kind of bad that I snapped at him.

"Theo, can you just pay attention for a few minutes?"

"It's hard. I'm hungry," he says simply.

I'm listening to the Astros vs Yankees game via livestream (Astros lead 7-1 in bottom of the 8th) when my phone buzzes. It's a text from Butch: *Coach Smith RETIRING!*

Coach Smith, from the high school? Wow. This *is* news. But I mean since Coach Smith is sort of ancient, maybe it's to be expected.

Hey, this could be okay actually. Get somebody new in there – somebody who doesn't know Coach Manton. Yeah, this could be a good thing. A very good thing.

I sit up in bed. My phone starts blowing

up. It's a group text with the entire Blaze team, something we've done periodically forever. They are all discussing this latest breaking baseball news. And in our world, believe me, this is a front page headline.

The texts are flying, but I don't chime in. I read them carefully, analyzing this development from every angle just like they are. There's a whole new power structure in the world of Welton baseball. Manton has always had an "in" with the high school that allows him to make or break someone's career before they even get there – but not anymore. Fresh blood means at least a chance for me.

Then Butch's comment beeps over my phone: *Maybe Pete Simmons will try out for the job. He's got nothing else going on.*

A couple of the guys quickly let Butch know I am part of this group text, and he sort-of-kind-of apologizes. I want to throw my phone but if I break it, I'll be out of luck and probably never get a new one – so I just slide it across the floor. It lands under my dresser. I see my phone vibrating amongst the cobwebs under there. I bury my face in a lumpy pillow.

The Yankees come back in the ninth and

beat the Astros, 8-7.

The first practice for Ash's team is like deja vu all over again. These guys are straight out of Garrido Little League: crummy equipment, no work ethic, no sense of urgency. Well, I came out of Garrido Little League too – but that was in another lifetime and I've moved on since then.

For the first ten minutes of practice, everyone is just laughing and talking. They all seem to know each other, except for me. I take care of my business, running and stretching and doing all the usual warm-ups. Even if I am doing it alone.

"Pete? Pete Simmons?"

This kid with the beginnings of a mustache is acting like he knows me.

"Yeah? I'm Pete..."

The kid turns and spits out a sunflower seed, then smiles at me. "It's me! Julio!"

Wow. The last time I saw Julio was the summer between fifth and sixth grades. He definitely did not have these bulging biceps back then.

"...Julio?"

"Yeah, man! What's happening? Great to

see you! I heard you were coming back!"

"Oh, I'm not back," I tell him.

"Oh..." Julio looks a little confused.

Just then, another guy says hello to Julio and as they are doing some sort of involved handshake, I walk away.

I get in the bullpen with Billy D, and once he gets warmed up, he is even better than I remember. He is over six feet already – but he's even skinnier than me. And funny thing is if you talk to him he definitely seems like he is barely 13, if that. His voice still sounds like a little kid. Maybe that's one reason he doesn't talk much and mostly keeps to himself. He just concentrates on throwing the ball. And I just concentrate on catching it. I feel comfortable with Billy D because I don't have to pretend to like all the shouting and laughing and fooling around the rest of the team is doing. He and I are the two quietest guys on the team, just putting in our work.

After I've been catching Billy D for about half an hour, I run the ball back to him. "When's Coach usually get here, anyway?" I ask.

He gives a nod out to center field, where a group of guys are shooting the breeze. It takes a second, but I realize one of those young guys *is* Coach. He's cut off all his dreadlocks and he is laughing along to some story that Julio is telling, just like everyone else.

"Great," I mutter. "When are we supposed to learn the signs?"

"We can make 'em up any way we want, I suppose."

"Really?"

Billy D nods. "Sure, you don't think Coach Key's going to call the pitches do you?"

That is exactly what I thought, but Billy D has just set me straight. I resume catching him and we work out a few signs and talk a little about how much and in what sequence he likes his pitches. He basically tells me he trusts my judgment completely though. Apparently he remembers me from some past tournaments, too. That kind of makes me feel good.

"What's going on?" It is Ash walking up behind me.

Billy D just nods and looks at me.

"Uh, just going over the signals, the different pitches, the game plan," I say. "We were...kind of...discussing...waiting for you..."

I stumble over my words like an idiot.

"That's up to you guys," Coach Ash says simply. "If you want to include me, great. But you can figure out the signs with the pitchers on your own, whatever feels right."

Okay, fine. I guess we are on our own here. Sink or swim, no help from him.

But I just say, "Yessir!"

Coach Ash gives me a fake military salute and kind of laughs, wandering off to talk with some other players.

After practice, I decide to take a run. If my parents are surprised, they don't say so. I never go running, but I want to start getting in better shape. For high school ball and all.

Who am I kidding?

I go up to the high school because I know that Livvie's soccer practice will be letting out in about half an hour. Did I mention that Livvie plays soccer in addition to volleyball? And she does cross country in the fall. She used to play basketball too and was invited to be on some elite travel team, but she couldn't find the time. Yeah...volleyball's her main sport but she's amazing at everything. One time Louie told me she was actually best at tennis, but she   won't do it because she only likes to play team sports.

I figure I can run the bleachers until her practice ends. And if Livvie and I just happen to run into each other afterward, it will be a coincidence.

Right.

Taking those metal steps on the bleachers two at a time, I start off cocky. On the way back down, I survey the stadium. The girls' team is at one end of the field, working on corner kicks. At the other end, a man is teaching his young son how to kick field goals through the uprights. Around the track a couple of clusters of moms stroll and chat.

By the third set of stairs, my heart is pounding and I am wishing I'd brought some water. Dumb mistake. I take the steps one at a time now, and place my foot carefully on each. When you get tired is when you get hurt, that is something Coach Manton always drills into us.

Or used to, anyway.

I see soccer practice breaking up, so I jog toward the far exit. I'll loop back around to-wards home through the parking lot, and if I run into her there it will seem even more random.

"What are you doing here?" Livvie's voice is genuinely mystified. "Does this new coach have you *running*?"

"Oh, hey Livvie. What's up?" My mouth is so parched, the words come out sounding even more tired than I really am. And I am pretty tired.

Livvie stares at me for a second then shakes her head.

"Here." She hands over her water jug.

"That's okay."

"I don't have cooties."

I smile at that. And grab the water jug and take a couple of wonderful, ice cold gulps.

"Remember cootie vaccinations? Belinda Carter drew them on everybody in 6th grade. For a dollar."

"She charged me two bucks!" Livvie says.

"That makes sense."

"And what is that supposed to mean?"

"Just that you probably needed the double dose."

"Because I was hanging out with you."

I squirt a little water on her. "But it was so worth it, right?"

"I guess. Since I never actually paid Belinda Carter the two dollars."

She heads toward the parking lot and I follow. We fall in rhythm, walking together companionably. She bumps her shoulder into mine, giving me "cooties." Then I bump my shoulder into hers.

She stops and checks the time on her phone. "Look...my dad's picking me up over there any minute. He and Louie will be here..."

"Oh yeah, okay. Well, I was just heading home..." I bump her shoulder again, but this time she doesn't reciprocate.

"Pete?"

"Yeah?"

"Did you really join another team?" She looks kind of hurt and confused. Or maybe just disgusted with me.

"Well, I...I guess." I think about that practice with Ash. If you can even call it a practice. All those guys – Julio and Billy D...I barely know them. They are just random people. Is that even a team? I think about my friends on the Texas Blaze and all the tour-

138

naments we've won. Three years of playing together. All those long hot practices and hard fought games...

"I mean, how could you just, like, abandon everybody?" asks Livvie.

"Wait, it wasn't like that. I didn't abandon them. I was just trying to defend..."

"Defend who?"

I see her dad's car pull into the parking lot. She does too.

"Okay, see you later!" Livvie's tone changes completely. She is urging me to go with a slightly panicked look in her eyes. I realize she really doesn't want her dad or her brother to see us together.

"Okay! Bye!!" she says.

The realization rocks me. Livvie Burns does not want to be seen with me.

I turn and jog away. My jog turns into a full out sprint. I run as fast as I can all the way home.

14

Theo and the other Little League players vote on a team name. We are the Lakers.

Yeah, I know. We tell them that's a basketball team. It doesn't matter. They want to be the Lakers.

I bring snacks this time. My mom got all emotional when I told her about Theo being hungry at practice, so she made 15 PB&Js and sent them with me. I am sort of embarrassed and think I will just leave them in my bag, but one kid actually *smells* them.

"What've you got in there? Is that peanut butter?"

Once I give him a sandwich, there is practically a stampede for every kid to get one. They gobble them down. I realize I can kind of relate. Nothing tastes as good as that afternoon snack, am I right?

Today's practice goes much better. I've brought some old musty catcher's equipment I found in our garage, leftover from my younger days. The catcher's gear has been repaired with duct tape more times than I can count, but it is still perfectly good for a 4' tall catcher. Arnie has gone to the Little League chapter office and they gave him a box of brand new balls, two bats and four batting helmets. A couple more kids bring gloves this time, and Zach has found a couple at Goodwill.

Hey, we are starting to look like a real team. I run the practice the structured way I've been taught. Long toss. Running. Stretching that always hurts me, but these kids seem able to bend into pretzels no problem. Base running drills. Fungo. Except we have no fungo bat, so that is just regular ground ball fielding. And then game situations.

It's kind of impossible to explain game situations to people who have never seen a game, so I keep it pretty basic. Like, hit the ball off the tee and run *that* way. I can't get over how many kids want to head straight to third.

Arnie and Zach cheer and encourage and praise God for all these great little players. I give a few tips here and there, telling a batter to choke up or a short stop to put his glove in the dirt. The kids soak it in. It's kind of amazing how you can tell them something once, and they'll do it every time. It makes me more careful with what I say.

We are taking a water break, everybody having a turn at an old concrete fountain where someone has spit their gum.

Theo comes up and leans against me. "Baseball is fun."

That hits me a little bit. I know it sounds stupid. But here we are with this crummy field and bad equipment and dirty water fountain...and yet to him, none of it matters. Baseball is fun. That kind of says it all. And didn't I have some great times on this very field myself, years ago?

"Can I put on the catch-up ear?" he asks.

"The catcher's gear? Sure," I tell him. I show him how to slip it on and strap it up. How to make sure the helmet is tight but not too tight. It actually fits him perfectly, with few adjustments.

"Pitch to me, pitch to me!" He is so excited.

In tee ball, of course there is no pitcher. The catcher's job is to stand back there in case someone ever throws a ball home for an out. Like that's going to happen with this team. But I throw him a few pitches anyway, just lob them in.

He is all excitement at first, but can't seem to actually catch one. Kind of important for a catcher to be able to catch.

"Don't reach for the ball, let it come to you," I intone, not sure if Theo is even listening. "Keep your hands soft, but your arm and wrist firm."

Another ball drops to the dirt.

"Theo! It's not that hard! Here, try again."

"Forget it..." he is watching some other boys play chase in the outfield.

"Let's not end on a dropped ball, one more pitch. Here you go...catch one!"

"I'm tired," he whines.

I figure maybe I was lobbing it so slowly that the ball didn't have enough oomph to land in his glove. A real pitch might actually be simpler – so I throw it right down the middle. A simple pitch, completely and easily catchable even by a little kid.

But at the moment I throw, Theo is distracted again by those dumb kids in the outfield and he takes his eye off the ball.

THWACK the ball hits him right in the side of the neck. I guess I threw it a little harder than I thought, because Theo goes sprawling backward and howls. I am the first one to him, and my adrenaline is pumping.

"Theo!"

It's such a relief when Theo springs up, looking mad. He isn't hurt too badly if he can do that.

"Hey! You hit me!" he pushes me backward, surprisingly hard. "That hurt!"

"You have to keep your eye on the ball there, buddy."

"I hate you! That hurt!"

"Look, Theo, it wasn't my fault. You have to keep your eye on the ball! That's the first rule of baseball."

I turn toward the kids goofing around in the outfield. "Hey! Come on! Pay attention and get to work out there!" My voice sounds funny yelling those words, but someone has to do it.

"Ouch..." Theo sticks out his lower lip, like the little kid he is.

"Hey, if you don't want to play baseball, you shouldn't be on the field."

I realize this is something Coach Manton has said to us dozens of times. Hundreds. And I always hated it. But that doesn't make it any less true. I mean, don't get on the field unless you're prepared to play, right?

By now, Arnie and Zach have come over to home plate to see if the kid is okay.

"He's fine," I tell them. "No big deal."

"Coach Pete threw a ball at me! I said I was tired and he wouldn't let me quit!"

By now all the boys are watching this exchange. Parents are arriving to pick up their kids.

Arnie intervenes. "Okay boys, let's get in a circle. Who wants to break it out?"

A dozen hands shoot in the air and all the boys clamor around Arnie. One of their favorite parts of practice is getting in a huddle. Everyone wants to be chosen to yell "TEAMWORK!" or "HUSTLE!" as they all throw their hands up. They can't get enough of it.

"Okay, Theo can break us out for the day..." Arnie announces.

I am not joining in because I am already gathering my equipment. I see my dad parked and waiting.

I hear Theo say, "No thanks. I just want to go home." He runs toward a big sister, or maybe it is his mom, who is walking up on the opposite side of the field, talking on her cell phone. As soon as he gets close to her, he bursts into tears and hugs her.

"What's wrong, little man?" she asks.

I slam the door of the car as I get in, interrupting Dad's reading of some stupid magazine.

"Oh! Hey." He starts the car. "How'd it go?"

I shrug and make a noncommittal sound.

"You hungry?" he asks. "Mom's making pasta."

At the dinner table that night, Mom tells me to quit texting. I am actually playing a game on my phone but I don't correct her. She has no idea that no one really texts me anymore. Certainly no one from the Texas Blaze. And I don't even have the phone number of anyone on my new team. Doesn't really matter, because I don't know them enough to contact them outside of practice anyway.

I sit on the front porch and watch people drive by in the twilight. It feels like the cars are all full of kids I maybe know, going to some get-together or movie or swimming pool that I might have been invited to... That is, if I hadn't quit the Texas Blaze. I guess I never realized how that team was like my entire social circle. It used to be that at practice somebody would say, "Wanna come over to my house later?" Or I'd get a text, "Let's go hit some balls in the cages and then go to the pool." But that doesn't happen anymore. Now I am just home. Alone. Bored.

I have really screwed up my life.

This sucks.

The summer stretches out in front of me. A total waste.

My phone buzzes. It is a text from Coach Ash. *Last minute, entered a tourney. triple play fields around 8a tomorrow. Hope u can come.*

And then he includes a link to some

YouTube video or something.

Hope you can come?

Forget that Ash is texting me the info. Forget that it is completely unprofessional to do this at the last minute. Forget it's less than twelve hours before the tournament. Forget that we don't even have uniforms. I don't even click on the video link. I don't even care about uniforms. Only one thing matters.

I am playing baseball tomorrow.

15

My dad parks right next to the Burns' SUV. The sight of the stickers for Livvie's soccer team and Livvie's volleyball team on the back window make my stomach lurch. Or maybe that is just the kolache I had for breakfast. Luckily Louie and his dad aren't in their car, so I don't have to see them. Yet.

My dad decides to sit in the car and read for awhile so I set off to look for my...teammates. Hard to think of Billy D and Julio like that, but whatever.

At a baseball tournament, you find out very quickly that when someone yells HEADS

UP you have to look around and cover your head – because that means a baseball just might be coming your way. The fields usually fan out in sets of four from a concrete block building in the middle that's the concession stand and bathrooms. So a foul pop up that goes over the backstop is going to fall in a very busy pedestrian area. I've seen so many near misses, I can't even tell you.

Big baseball tournaments usually have a kind of carnival atmosphere – complete with county fair food like funnel cakes sprinkled in powdered sugar and frito pies with chili and jalapenos. There are often a few tables set up selling things like beaded bracelets that say BASEBALL GRANDMA or airbrushed t-shirts where you can get your team name written like graffiti. And amidst everything, you can usually find dozens of little kids running around playing chase and drinking soda.

There are all kinds of baseball fans in this world, but some of the parents who come to these weekend tournaments can be divided into three basic kinds: Cheerers, Chewers and City Folk.

The Cheerers are the big extended families who really camp out and bring lots of food from home, usually even setting up tables and little pop up tents. These families are committed to their teams. It's like a fulltime hobby or something. They make a tailgating day out of it, with grandparents, aunts and uncles wearing matching t-shirts. Sometimes they have the fancy folding chairs with a footrest, an umbrella and a drink-holder built in. These super-fan families are often the most vocal fans, if you know what I mean – they cheer the loudest but they are also super hard on their own sons. They don't hesitate to criticize their own team, or any other one. Lemme tell you, the catcher hears pretty much every comment.

Next, there are the country people. These are families who drive in from small towns hours away. The men usually have dark tans from working out in the hot Texas sun in one job or another, and they wear jeans no matter the weather. This group can be pretty reserved – they don't cheer much and never boo. The women bring folding chairs and sit in a line right up against the fence, talking quietly among themselves and holding tiny portable electric fans. The men pace a ways back and eat seeds or chew tobacco. That's why I call this group the Chewers.

Lastly, there are the City Folk – such as

the Texas Blaze crowd. These parents do not wear team colors, unless you count their fancy university sweatshirts or the baseball caps from Vail or Napa. They sport gigantic to-go coffee mugs and perch on the top rows of the bleachers texting updates to some busy people who couldn't make the game. This group sends up a lot of congratulatory cheers and optimistic encouragement at the smallest thing. They are also much more indignant at anything they perceive as slightly unfair by the umps. I guess they aren't as used to dealing with any kind of injustice – they're absolutely aghast at the idea their kids might face unfairness. And City Folk are usually the quickest to play the money card – you know what I mean: "Hey, we're paying good money for this!" I'm always thinking the money can't mean that much to them, but I guess that's what it comes down to for rich people. They are used to being in charge because they have the money to back it up.

I'm not sure where my new "team" will fit into this hierarchy, probably None of the Above. I am just hoping it won't be a gigantic group of Cheerers. I walk around looking for someone else that's playing for Ash. I know the Texas Blaze always congregates by the west batting cages on mornings like this, so I head the other way. The tournament bracket is posted next to the snack bar, so out of habit I walk up to check it. It hits me – I don't even know our team name. But it isn't hard to figure out: the Ashafarians.

Why?

Please help me.

And first game of the day? None other than the Slammers. The team that gave us so much trouble last time we were here. Well, not "us," but gave the Blaze so much trouble.

"Hey hey hey, it's Pete Simmons!" somebody yells. It is Tom Murphy, a fellow...Ashafarian.

"Hi, Tom. Where's everybody?"

"Not sure. Listen, can I borrow a couple of bucks? My parents dropped me off and they're coming later, but I wanna get a breakfast taco. I'll pay you back."

I know I'll never see that five dollars again. And that leaves me with only three bucks for the rest of the day unless I ask my dad for more, which I hate to do.

I finally find Coach Ash and the guys over at the east cages. They are all joking about how we are probably going to get killed by the

Slammers. Real hilarious. Coach Ash has brought a roll of duct tape (my dad would be so happy) and is taping makeshift jersey numbers on the back of everybody's t-shirt. He makes me 11. That was my number on the Blaze, but I haven't told Ash that. Maybe it is just a good guess on his part. Anyway, I don't really talk to anybody, just take care of my business and get my equipment in order for the upcoming game.

Tom joins us, mouth full of taco. "What do we know about the Slammers, anyway?"

"We know they beat the Blaze!" says Coach Ash.

Everybody gets a laugh out of that. Except me, of course,

Coach Ash squats among us. He grabs a handful of Isaac's sunflower seeds, and pops a few in his mouth.

"Hey!" Isaac protests.

"I take my payment in seeds and gum and Gatorade. Everybody take note, I'll be expecting snacks on a regular basis." He spits a couple of shells on the ground.

Come to think of it, how are we paying coach? On the Blaze, parents were always handing coach their monthly checks or getting reminders that their fees were due at the end of a tournament. I haven't heard one word about money from Ash.

Tom finishes his breakfast taco in one giant bite and makes the foil wrapper into a ball. "What's with this Ash-far-ities?"

The other guys laugh.

"Ashafarians...sorry, guys, best I could do on short notice." Coach Ash laughs too. "I was tired when they called and asked us to play – some other team cancelled and the tournament director is a friend of mine..."

"Well, the name sucks!" says Isaac. Some of the other players agree.

"Alright, alright, what can I say? It was late and I was listening to Bob Marley! We'll change it for the next tournament."

Coach Ash doesn't even seem to care that everyone's making fun of the name. That everyone's disrespecting him.

"So what's the batting order?" a shortstop named Casey asks.

This Casey guy seems kind of green to me, and this proves it. You *never* ask the coach the batting order, or anything about the plan for the game. The coaches keep it in their heads and give it out to you as necessary. Everybody knows that.

Ash waves hello to some old guy walking by, and then the wave turns into a huge stretch. "I don't know, Casey. How about you leading off?"

"No, man! That's what I'm talking about, I told you it's too much pressure!" Casey is indignant.

"Okay, okay, I'll get Pete to do it," laughs Coach.

"Which one's Pete?" Isaac asks. I think he knows my name, but wants to pretend he doesn't.

Coach claps my shoulder. "Right here, Pete Simmons!"

"You know, the rich white kid that used to play on the Blaze," chimes in Tom.

What's funny is not just that they think I'm rich – but that Tom is also white, like half the guys on this stupid team. Anyway, all the guys get a big laugh at my expense, especially Julio.

"You up for leading off, Simmons?" Coach Ash asks.

"Yessir!" I retie my left cleat, even though it doesn't need it.

16

Amazing but true: we win our first three games. The Slammers' best pitcher and their short stop have both gone on family vacations, so we manage to get lucky. And the third team we play looked like 12U. How we get these matchups, I'm not sure – but I think Ash must be friends with somebody. What am I saying? Ash is friends with everybody, even if he's never met them before. He played plenty of tournaments around here back in the day, apparently. Before he headed off to college in the Northeast, he played with a bunch of different select summer ball teams all around Central Texas. And despite changing teams often, he seems to have left no enemies in his wake. Coach Manton would never put up with that sort of disloyalty. Come to think of it, I guess that's why Manton never mentioned Ash.

It's been a long day and our semifinal game is 9am tomorrow morning and I should head straight home to ice my thumb and rest up. Catching every inning of three games in this sticky humidity takes it out of me, although I have to admit the innings were pretty quick. The Ash-a-whatevers apparently have some pretty big beginner's luck.

My dad heads for the car, taking my bag and water jug. I tell him I am just going to the snack bar and I'll be right behind him. He says, no hurry.

I pass Julio who says, "Good game today!" and looks like he wants to talk, but I just say "Good game," and keep walking.

I kind of want to stop by Field Three before I leave. It's the qualifying game for the other semifinals slot, so the winner here is who we will be playing tomorrow morning. I just want to check the score...

Blaze are up by one run, 6-5 in the bottom of the fifth. I walk up just as a ball rolls under Butch's mitt at first base. What's Butch doing at first anyway? Manton must be trying out some new things. Butch recovers quickly and chases the ball down, but when he turns to flip the ball to first, no one is covering the base. Since he's the pitcher, Louie should be there. It's a stupid mistake, am I right? I mean, covering first is something I was just teaching the Little League Lakers at their practice.

"What the hell!" The familiar sound of Coach Manton yelling. "Lou Burns! Where were you?!"

Louie goes back to the mound, trying not to listen. Getting too caught up in Coach Manton's tirades is a great way to lose your concentration and confidence, and then your game is shot for at least the rest of the inning. I know that well. All of us on the Blaze do.

Not that I'm on the Blaze anymore.

"We got the tying run on second and two outs and you don't cover first base?!" Manton takes a couple steps out onto the field. The ump could call him for that, but the guy pretends not to notice and takes the opportunity to go have a drink from the water bottle he's stashed in the other team's dugout.

"I will take you out of there so fast, it'll make your head spin! I'll get somebody in there who can field the position, goddamn it!"

Since the umpire is taking an unofficial time out, Louie now has nothing to do but stand there and take the public reaming indifferently. His passive coolness doesn't fool me. I see Livvie in the stands, shifting in her seat.

So she *is* here. I've been keeping an eye out for her all day, but never caught a glimpse. I figured she had a tournament out of town and wasn't going to show up, but looks like she is here now... Fresh from soccer, still in her jersey and shorts, with her hair in a braid and rosy cheeks from a long day out on the field. Or maybe her face is turning pink listening to Coach yell at her brother.

Mr. and Mrs. Burns are chatting with friends, ignoring Manton's insults toward their son. Actually, most of the Texas Blaze parents are laughing and talking among themselves, probably feeling that it's more polite not to watch the public humiliation. It seems like Livvie and I are the only ones with the guts to watch Louie get chewed out.

"Show me something out there, Burns! Show me you've got something, *anything*, because right now I don't see it! Nothing! You got nothing! Do you hear me? HUH?"

The Blaze have a new catcher, not Bellows but someone I've seen on the Twisters before. The Twisters are a team that never wins much. They are one of those developmental programs that are all about personal growth and training. You know, lots of scrimmages and arm-band workouts and lectures but not too many actual games. I hear they have homework – worksheets and essays on visualizing baseball success. To tell you the truth, that doesn't sound so bad to me, but all the other guys make fun of it. Anyway, I'm sure this kid jumped at the chance to switch to the Blaze and maybe win a couple of tournaments.

Ball, outside.

"You've got one more pitch to show me something, Burns, or you're out of there!" The threats from the dugout are so pointed and harsh and loud, how can a pitcher – or any ball player – keep his concentration? But none of the parents or other teammates react at all. For some reason it pops into my mind how Ash would probably react. He wouldn't sit with a stoneface like everyone else. He'd probably crack a joke or something, knowing him. I'm still not sure if Ash really takes baseball seriously.

Ball, way outside. The new catcher from

the Twisters can't even get a glove on it, though he lays out for it, diving in the dirt, giving it his best try. The runners on first and second easily advance a base. Manton takes off his hat and jumps around in a little circle, as if he's looking for something good to hit or kick but can't find anything.

"Burns, you're out of there!" Manton screams. People on the next field can probably hear him.

I see Livvie cup her hands to her mouth and "BOOOOOOOOOO!" in a deep voice. Her mother swats her hands down and glares. Livvie quietly argues with her mother a bit, probably saying she is just defending her brother or something like that... Anyway, they whisper back and forth and pretty soon Livvie gets up in a huff and starts heading my way. I know she doesn't expect to see me.

I turn my eyes to Louie, as he sinks onto the bench and gets the full wrath of Manton's diatribe up close and personal.

"What are you doing here?!" Livvie sounds angry. I hope she is just keyed up over the game, and not mad at me.

"Just watching."

"Why? You scouting, so you can tell your new team all about it?!" I guess she is angry with me, or at least taking it out on me.

"Sucks they took Louie out."

"Like you care. Now you can be right – yeah, Coach Manton's such a jerk! *See, I told you so!*"

I hate hearing her impersonation of me. And I am not really thinking 'I told you so.'

Much.

I don't want to fight with Livvie so I just say, "See you later" as I walk away.

Of course I'd been hoping I'd run into her today but this is not at all what I'd imagined. At this point, I just don't want to make her any angrier than she already is. I mean, the one time I see her, we fight? Better to walk away. Besides, my dad is still waiting.

But Livvie is hot on my heels. "Where are you going? Too good to talk to me now?"

I speed up. I am practically jogging to get away from her but she stays right with me.

"You just look down your nose at everybody, huh? Well, problems don't disappear just because you run away!" she is almost shouting at me.

"I didn't say that!"

"I know you think you're so superior now, but I think you're just disloyal!"

We are out in the dark of the parking lot when I spin around.

"You know that's not true!" I tell her.

She grabs my arm and pushes – but doesn't let go of me. It is kind of like that time behind the barbecue place. Two forces coming at each other, colliding. Or attracting. Or something magnetic. You know how when you hold two magnets, they re-pel/attract/repel depending on which way you hold the magnets? It was like that.

When I finally kiss her, she doesn't pull away. At least not at first.

"You know, I didn't have a choice," I whisper to her. "You think I wanted to leave? I was just trying to do the right thing."

My heart is beating all the way into my fingertips, and I think she can probably feel it in my hands on her shoulders.

"You always have a choice," she doesn't sound so mad anymore. Just kind of sad and tired.

I don't know what to say to that. All I know is I don't want to destroy this moment. Just being close to her, without yelling or fighting, is enough.

I lean in again, without realizing it is happening. My lips on hers.

"No," she pushes my chest. Right in the same spot that Coach Manton kneed me, in the solar plexus. "I have to go check on Louie. Make sure he's okay."

We both know that she can't go talk to Louie, as he will still be in the dugout and Manton forbids players from talking to anybody during a game. I don't care if your great-grandmother comes for a visit and brings Buster Posey with her, it is eyes-on-the-field and head-in-the-game at all times.

"Well...okay...bye."

She turns and walks away. I see the lights for one of the fields go off, then another. Only the Texas Blaze game is still going on.

"Meet me on the corner, by that playground place with the seesaw things!" I yell after her. "Tonight!" I run after her a few steps. "I'll be there around eleven!"

A family walking by looks at me. The woman gives me squinty-eyed suspicion but the son smiles. The dad burps.

Livvie doesn't turn around, or act like she hears me at all.

17

My parents practically insist on taking me out to dinner, even though it is late and I am tired and I have a game tomorrow morning and... Okay, really all I want is to get the folks to fall asleep as early as possible so I can sneak out and go to the playground, where I will no doubt wait alone in the dark because Livvie will be a no-show. Still, being stood up by her will be the most exciting Saturday night I've had in weeks.

I decide a restaurant with the 'rents might be quicker anyway, because Mom won't be up doing dishes and puttering in the kitchen until late, so I agree to go out. Listen to me, like I'm doing them a favor by letting them take me to dinner. But I kind of am, because who wants to be seen out with their parents on a Saturday night? I sort of hint as much, if you call a hint saying, "We're not going any place in our neighborhood, are we?" But turns out we aren't, we are heading to East Austin to this little Mexican place where Mom has been having lunch a lot, Takoba. She says they serve authentic native cuisine.

Oh great.

But once I get there and see we are going to sit outside in this cool patio area with plastic chairs around big wooden spools and Christmas lights hanging from the trees, I realize maybe this will be kind of okay. Plus all the smells are making me hungry. There is a guy in the corner playing guitar and singing, but he doesn't have a microphone or anything. In Austin, you can never be certain if it's the evening's official entertainment, or just a guy waiting for his tacos.

The tortilla chips are thick and homemade, still hot from the fryer with lots of salt. I scoop up the mild green salsa by the tablespoonful and wash it all down with limeade. My mom recommends the combo platter and it does not disappoint: a gooey cheesy enchilada, a crispy chalupa piled high with chicken and lettuce and homegrown tomatoes, alongside big helpings of rice and beans.

My dad tells this long involved story about how the soccer officials in Europe are being investigated for cheating in some big gambling scandal masterminded by the Chinese mafia. A baby at the next table keeps smiling at me and playing peek-a-boo. The guy with the guitar takes a request from a grey-haired hippie and plays something catchy. It sounds vaguely familiar, and it must be a golden oldie because my parents start swaying to the music and humming along. The baby throws tortilla chips on the ground and laughs. Her parents don't get mad, they just shrug and smile at me.

By the time I get home with a full belly and that old song stuck in my head, I've almost convinced myself that Livvie might actually meet me at the playground. After all, it is a beautiful summer night and she hadn't said no. Of course, she hadn't said yes. Actually, I wasn't even sure if she'd heard me.

It is 10:20 when my mother rouses my sleeping father from the couch and turns off all the lights. I give it another fifteen minutes and then go out the front door, the one furthest from their room. I wouldn't call it sneaking out exactly, because I am leaving a note on my bed. I don't want them to worry or anything, I just tell them that I've decided to go meet Livvie at the park... I think they'd be happy about that actually, even if it does mean walking alone through a neighborhood with no street lights in the middle of the night.

My mom was instrumental in voting down the road lamps, since it messes with wildlife and creates light pollution that stops all of us from seeing the stars, not to mention uses up energy. She fought the issue valiantly on several occasions, practicing her arguments on Dad and me a few times. I became totally convinced – street lights are a bad idea.

Unless you are out walking at night. Alone.

I make it to the playground. It is this little homeowners' park in a fancy community just a couple of streets over. The neighborhood changes fast from the rental duplexes we live in to the swimming-pool-and-sport-court crowd over here. I never feel as comfortable in this area, but at least the roads and yards are lit.

The little park has a wrought iron fence that I can step right over. I guess it was built to keep little kids from running in the street or something. I climb the ladder slide to get a better view down the hill. No one is coming. There's not a sound or a movement any-where. 11:03pm. I hope she hasn't come and left already. She could've come early and then given up.

Who am I kidding?

She's not coming.

I walk on the teeter-totter, back and forth from one side to the other, balancing as the side I am on always goes down. Too easy. I decide to do a handstand right in the center, keeping the seesaw in a flat stance, parallel to the ground. It takes a couple of tries, but I finally balance just right and get it steady. I wish somebody could take a picture or some-thing, because it is pretty cool... but after I hold it for a few long seconds, I just hop down.

Still alone.

Maybe this is kind of a weird place to meet someone in the middle of the night. Maybe Livvie didn't even know what I was talking about... but I think she does. We came here one time when I was over visiting Louie and his dog got out. Livvie and I had both dashed out to catch her and we had to chase her all the way here. We wound up hanging out for awhile, goofing around on the seesaws and stuff. That was a long time ago. But she probably remembers. Maybe. Or not.

I sit on a swing but don't push off. I just hang, still in the night, thinking about how maybe after this summer season is over, I can be back with all my friends and we will all be on the high school team and we'll never have to discuss all of this again. Put it behind us. And everything will be normal again. Especially with Livvie.

There is a rustling in a hedge about thirty feet away, and I think it's Livvie but believe it or not, a little reddish brown fox comes walking out. I don't know if it is a baby or they are always that size, but the fox is smaller than a house cat with a tail fluffier and bigger around than his whole body. He walks and sniffs, not a care in the world apparently. He catches a scent once, and lifts his nose in the night breeze... but I guess it isn't an interesting smell because he soon starts nosing around the grass again. I watch until he is about a hundred yards away.

I somehow don't hear Livvie's footsteps until she is quite close. Maybe she tiptoed, who knows. That way she could always turn around and run away if she changed her mind about coming. But I see her before that can happen... I smile but she doesn't.

Livvie has a little more trouble than I did stepping over the wrought iron fence, but she manages. I try to keep my face neutral and my body relaxed, even as I feel the adrenaline coursing through my veins at the sight of her.

She really has come to meet me. I can't believe it.

She looks so beautiful in the blue light of the night, with her curls windblown around her face. I am so happy to see her, I don't even care if she is maybe planning to ream me out. But I'd kind of prefer if she doesn't.

"Hey, Livvie."

She sits down in the swing next to me.

She starts pumping her legs, getting the swing going. I follow suit, gently swinging my legs back and forth.

The moment feels delicate. Livvie is more skittish than the fox, and I move deliberately, careful not to spook her. We swing, but not in unison.

"I'll bet I can touch that branch with my toe," Livvie challenges. She begins to swing higher.

"No way," I pump my legs harder.

"Yes way."

"It's impossible to reach that."

"Yeah, that's right. Too hard for you, Simmons. Don't even try." There is a smile behind her voice.

We are both swinging in earnest now, racing to make contact with that elusive tree branch hanging overhead.

"You scared of a little competition, Liv?" I shoot back.

I see the glint of her teeth as she smiles. "Hardly."

We are each getting closer to the branch.

"Come on..." I concentrate, pumping in earnest.

"Wait a minute, your swing is closer!" Livvie says.

"No, it's n—well, yeah okay maybe a little closer."

"Uh huh! And your legs are longer," she complains.

She pushes me gently in mid-air, setting me slightly off-course. Our swings are going precariously high, and I think she loves it as much as I do. As we reach the top of each arc, the swing chains go slack for just a second and we lift out of our seats and for a moment are just suspended there... then *drop* back down and up again.

As our swinging synchronizes, the metal swing-set begins to rock ever so slightly, upping the danger quotient.

"Almost..." Liv is getting really close.

I pump my whole body, and inch forward in the seat of my swing and point my toe –

Just as Livvie pushes it higher than ever –

Her foot brushes the branch.

And the swing-set lurches forward violently, scaring us both. We jump out of our swings mid-air, landing together on the ground in a jumble.

"Are you okay?" In this moment, Livvie isn't trying to hide her concern for me.

"I'm fine, are you okay?"

Livvie leans back. "You almost got us hurt with your crazy idea."

"My idea?" I throw a little pebble at her leg. "You're just mad because you didn't win."

"What?! I did win!"

The headlights of a passing car send us behind the hedge.

"What is somebody doing out now? It's almost midnight," I whisper.

"Yeah, who would be crazy enough to be out in this neighborhood at midnight." She smiles.

"Remember Mrs. Phelps?"

That's our old Food Sciences teacher who lives right down the street.

"Oh yeah! Mrs. Phelps. Is she a lesbian?"

"What?! No!"

"Why, there's not anything wrong with it," says Livvie.

"True," I admit. "But still."

Livvie laughs. "What made you think of her?"

"I just like her. At Halloween, she gave out dollar bills. She didn't have any candy. She said she'd forgotten it was Halloween! That blew my 11-year-old mind. How do you forget Halloween?"

"I kind of think Mrs. Phelps looks like Spongebob."

"She does always wear a belt," I agree.

We are close to each other, and her smile is so natural and open. It makes me feel like we are in seventh grade and everything is still perfect and uncomplicated and we just won the Fall Slugfest.

I move to kiss her again, but she ducks her head. "I have to get back. Louie was still up playing video games in his room when I left."

"It's not like he's going to come tell you goodnight or anything."

"I know, but still..."

I do know. We both need to get home. But I want to thank her for coming to see me. Or something. I just... want to tell her how I feel. And if I knew, I would tell her.

I squeeze her hand real quick.

"Race you to the end of the street!" That is where our paths will divide, right by the Burns' house. "Double or nothing on that swinging thing," I add.

But Livvie doesn't run, so neither do I. We just walk down the street together, slowly. For the first time in weeks, I feel a weight lifting. Even if I can just have one friend, just Livvie, it will be enough to get me through the summer.

"Listen, Pete, I have to tell you something."

Okay, I guess we are going to get serious. I can do that.

"Livvie, I know everybody's mad at me or whatever, because I quit, but you know what? I just didn't feel like I had a choice. I mean, Manton was basically about to kill somebody. Why should we put up with the way he is sometimes?"

I can hear myself talking, and it's like I am realizing this as I am saying it. Now that my ideas are being put into words and spoken out loud, I am gaining confidence. You know what, I am kind of right! Why should we put up with Manton's temper?

"Pete..."

I barrel on. "It's just not right. He screams, he pushes, he... Let's face it, there's no reason to put up with it. I know Louie hates it too. And Butch. All the guys do. We need to stand up for ourselves and remember why we love baseball, why we even want to play in the first pl-"

"Pete."

"What?"

She looks like she might cry or some-

180

thing.

"I'm sorry, Livvie-"

"No, it's not you. I'm the one who's sorry."

"What is it?"

We have come to our parting corner. I'm not sure why everything is so sad all the sudden.

"Livvie? Are you okay? I didn't mean to say that about Manton...he's not so bad."

"Yes, he is!" She turns and runs.

I watch her until she goes all the way into her house. I see the light still on in Louie's room.

After a few seconds, I turn toward home. I'd better get back in my bed and get ready for the tournament tomorrow. I don't know why Livvie looked like she was about to cry, but her emotion tells me one thing.

She still cares.

18

I arrive at the fields a full hour and ten minutes before our Sunday morning game, even though I know no one else on the team will be following that protocol. The habit is just too ingrained to break. Manton's rule is always be there an hour beforehand, and everyone knows "on time is ten minutes late" so hence my early arrival. I won't say I'm superstitious, but I'm a baseball player. Habits and rituals are important.

And of course I want to see the bracket right away and find out who we are playing. They hadn't posted it online last night and I didn't think to ask Livvie, so I still wasn't sure who had qualified for the semifinal game. I go to where the paper had been taped on the wall yesterday. There it is, plain as day: Blaze vs Ashafarians.

I knew it.

Some kid has scrawled in pencil right next to Ashafarians, "SUX!" We do kind of suck, so I don't pay it much mind. I can't even believe we've made it to the semifinals.

I prepare to get creamed by all of my old teammates. The inevitability of the loss is strangely relaxing. Somehow, I feel like this game might set everything right and be a sort of deserved punishment for me. Maybe Louie and Butch and Richard will not be quite as mad at me if they can take out their anger on the field by beating us silly.

The taped-on numbers of my "uniform" are starting to peel off since my mom washed it last night. I push them back on, knowing it only has to last for one more game.

It's cloudy and a few raindrops fall here and there, but the gusts of wind dry them pretty quickly. Anytime you walk up to a field on a cold or wet morning, you are usually greeted by a dad – or two, or five – with their classic comment, "Great baseball weather!" Or my favorite, "Perfect day for baseball!" Was that ever a funny line? I stop to watch an 8U game, the little kids in their sparkling clean uniforms. Neither team is that great, I feel like my Lakers could take them, although who am I kidding. The Lakers have never even played a game. Still, we do have some talent on the field, I am seeing it more and more every practice.

The 8U coach pulls his bucket out of the dugout and plants himself in the sightline of the catcher. I don't know who the genius is that started selling buckets of balls with a padded top, but I'm sure they've made a few bucks. I'm wondering what this coach is going to do out there, is he seriously calling pitches? I mean how many eight-year-olds have a curve or a breaking ball?

I am enjoying the little kids' game, feeling almost...relaxed? On a game day? How is that possible? It's probably because I already know the Ashafarians are going to lose, but maybe it is also because I can still hear Livvie laughing while we were swinging last night. And because I know Coach Ash is not going to yell at me today, no matter how badly I screw up. Whatever it is, I just enjoy the feeling.

I head off to find my team. Even the Ashafarians should be showing up by now. I round the corner to see the Blaze warming up at the west cages. Like clockwork, with their well-practiced drills.

Louie is making Butch laugh about something when he glances over and sees me.

"Hey Simmons," Butch yells.

"Hey," I answer.

"What are you doing here?" Louie asks, although I am pretty sure he knows.

"Gonna play you guys."

Louie and Butch exchange a look and a laugh.

"That'll be fun...for us," says Butch. "What is Ash-a-*fart*-ian, anyway?"

"That's French for 'I can't play baseball'" Louie chimes in.

Even I have to laugh. A little.

A stray ball comes rolling in from the guys warming up nearby. I lean down and pick it up. Louie walks toward me. Butch heads toward me too.

In a lowered voice Louie says, "You hear about the coach at the high school?"

"Yeah, he's leaving or something..." I take a step toward them. This is good. We are just going to talk, like normal.

"Yeah, Smith left, but they found a replacement," Louie smiles.

"Oh yeah?"

This is great. Louie is thinking about next year just like I am. The guys are looking forward to the time we can all play together again, like we have for the past three years. It is all going to be back to normal very soon.

Butch says, "Yeah! My dad heard about it from a friend of his on the school board. They had the interview on Friday."

Louie's smile doesn't look friendly all the sudden. "Yep. Looks like Manton's got the job," he says.

Louie holds his glove out, wanting me to throw him the baseball.

Don't react, just stay cool. That is my main thought. I guess all the other thoughts are floating around in there, too: I've ruined my chances at high school baseball... Manton will be the high school coach and he'll never put me on a team... Butch and Louie were so anxious to tell me this... Now I'll never make a decent team again... I'm not going to get to play with my friends ever... And this must be what Livvie was wanting to tell me

187

last night – and it's probably the only reason she was nice to me last night, because she felt sorry for me... And now I am going to have to play these guys in a game, play against Manton, knowing that my career is over... Knowing that no matter the outcome of this game, the Texas Blaze have just won....forever.

All of those thoughts are a confused jumble running through my brain. But my main emotion is: Just. Be. Cool.

I turn and head for the east batting cages. More clouds are rolling in, getting darker now. A perfect day for baseball.

"Simmons! That's our ball!" Butch shouts after me.

I turn and toss it right into Louie's glove, just like I have a thousand times before.

By the time I've gone through the motions of warming up with the Ashafarian team, I no longer have to fight back tears. They are long gone. Somehow I kick into this gear of intense adrenaline combined with total calm. It is like a bubble surrounds me and nothing much matters. As my Uncle Luke always jokes, "Keep it surreal." I'm experiencing everything around me like it's a movie with the sound down. Out of habit, I direct my teammates on what to do, organizing them to take turns in the cages while I hit ground balls to warm up the infielders.

Coach Ash shows up just in time for the coin toss, and he wins it so we are the home team. He is his usual loose self, humming some song that is popular on the radio and doing a little dance step as he comes into the dugout.

"Let's see it, Billy D! I know you got moves," Ash tells him.

There's no way Billy D is going to get up and dance but Julio is not afraid to bust it out. He does moves like the robot and the sprinkler.

"Okay, who's got the seeds?" Ash demands. "Tom? What's in your mouth?"

Tom brings out his bag of sunflower seeds and pours a few into Ash's open palm.

"Seeing as you just showed up, thought you'd have had enough time to stop and buy your own today."

Wait, did I just think that to myself, or did I actually say it out loud?

"Ooooooooooo, you got burned!" Some of the other players are laughing at Ash. A couple of them throw sunflower seeds at him. "Buy your own, Coach! Snap!"

Ash stares at me. I don't even tense up. Right now, nothing can get through my bubble of not caring, of this hopeless situation. What does anything matter?

Ash starts laughing and claps me on the shoulder a couple of times. "I knew I liked you. You remind me of when I was young and stupid."

Okay, maybe that is the one thing that can break through the bubble. A pat on the back.

"You're alright, kid." Ash looks deep into my eyes, as if he knows what is going on. "You're going to be fine."

He squeezes my shoulder and turns toward the field. "Let's do this! Isaac, you wanna play second today?"

I swallow hard, and put on my catcher's mask.

My old friend, the catcher's mask, that protects me in times good and bad. I've been meaning to clean all the dust and old sweat off of it. Won't need to do that now. This will probably be the last time I'll use it.

"And Pete?" Ash asks.

I turn toward him. "Yeah?"

"I notice you use a different bat for the games than when you do BP. I like that. Good idea."

And Ash trots out of the dugout.

Since it is semi-finals they have an announcer for the game, just a guy with a microphone who sits on a platform behind homeplate and operates the scoreboard. He must have been a frustrated radio announcer, because he really puts his heart into it. When he says my name I think, "This may be the last time I hear myself announced over a loudspeaker in a baseball game."

The announcer guy turns on this battery operated boombox and plays a scratchy recording of the National Anthem. I put my hand over my heart and stand in a crooked line with the rest of the Ashafarians. I try not to look at Mr. and Mrs. Burns and Mr. Loezier and the rest of the Texas Blaze parents in the stands.

The whole experience takes on a weird edge, as if I'm looking back into my past and missing it. It's like these are already the good ol' days – back when I used to play baseball.

I have to stop thinking like this. *Shake it off, Simmons!*

I crouch behind the plate and Billy D throws a few warm-up pitches. Just concentrate on the ball and you'll be fine, I tell myself.

Louie has become the Blaze's lead off hitter now that I'm gone. He doesn't look at me or acknowledge me at all, just steps up to the plate like he owns it. Billy D has his usual calm exterior, but I can tell he is nervous on the inside. Actually I guess the whole ballpark can tell he is nervous on the inside, because he throws the first pitch about six feet over my head. I have to spring *way* up to grab it.

"Nice stop, catcher!" I hear my dad's comment loud and clear among all the others. It's a pointless thing to say really, because it doesn't matter if I stop the ball or not since no one's on base. Still, it's nice to hear.

When my dad cheers for me at a game, he always calls me "catcher" or "number eleven." I've never told him before, but I like that. It is a lot less embarrassing than the parents who yell out childhood nicknames during key moments of the game: "Catch it, Mikey!" or

"Run, Jellybean, run!" Those are real examples, by the way. In 5th grade, there was a grandmother who cheered long and loud all season for "Jellybean." Poor Johnny Garcia. He eventually just quit the game of baseball altogether, even though he jacked three homeruns that season and was a decent 2nd baseman. I have to blame Grandma.

The next pitch, I call for Billy D's curve. It's his best pitch, and it's pretty nasty. Let's show the Blaze what we got, I'm thinking. Let's play bold. I mean now or never, right?

Billy D throws the ball perfectly and it comes in with a lot of movement. But Louie is ready for it – I'm sure Manton's had somebody scout out the Ashafarians, even though yesterday is the first time we've played together as a team. No threat is too small to escape Manton's attention. That's what makes him so good, I guess.

Louie swings and makes huge contact, crushing the ball to right field. My old Little League teammate Julio doesn't make the catch and Louie makes it to first base. Easily.

Billy D manages to strike out Bellows, bringing up Richard. I can't believe Richard Loezier is now batting third, as he rarely gets on base. But hey, what do I know anymore?

Richard tries to give me a nod hello, but I pretend the ball is muddy and I exchange it for a new one from the ump. I crouch into position and give Billy D the signal for a fast ball. He throws three in a row, striking out Richard with ease. He never even swings. Louie keeps trying to steal on me but I pop up and jump out every time, staring him down. He stays on first.

Next up is Butch. He's batted clean-up as long as I can remember, and he's good at it. I signal to Billy D for a change-up. Butch won't be expecting that for his first pitch.

My plan doesn't work. The sound of the impact rings in my ears and the world switches to slo-mo. HD slo-mo. There is nothing to do but watch Butch's baseball sail up and out, with Julio scrambling to get there. Louie is already rounding second, since everybody runs with two outs. And I'm pretty sure Louie will try to head for me if that ball drops – I know Manton will send him, and that collision at home plate won't be pretty. Julio's not going to get there in time to make the catch. The ball is coming down and – maybe a breeze catches it? – the ball falls just outside the white line.

"FOUL!" yells the ump.

Butch trots back to home plate and picks up his bat. Louie re-sets to first. I try to breathe normally.

Next I call a knuckleball. I figure Butch won't be expecting that either, and this time it works. Butch pops it straight up over our heads, and I throw off my mask. The runner is supposed to get out of my way, but Butch kind of lingers around home plate before he takes off. That's okay, I can see the ball clear as day against the grey clouds, spinning with those red laces going round and round. It is coming back down now, and I shuffle backward to align myself. This will be the third out and then I'm first up for the Ashafarians. I'm pretty sure Louie will be pitching, I saw him in the bullpen earlier. I can't think about that – first make this catch. The ball shifts in the wind and I adjust, getting my glove into perfect position to catch that baseball. I take one more step backward, and just as the ball lands in my mitt, I felt a hot flash of pain in my left ankle.

I land on my tailbone, hard. I hear the crowd and the players give a collective little gasp of breath.

"Petey!" my dad yells.

I guess he is prone to those childhood nicknames after all, but right now I don't care. Between my ankle and my tailbone, I am living in a world of pain.

Ash runs out of the dugout. Billy D runs in from the mound. I see Coach Manton over in the third base box, chatting with Louie, not a care in the world.

I hold up my mitt to the ump. I still have the ball.

"OUT!" he yells.

"What?? You can't do that!" screams Manton, now jumping into action. "It was a dead ball! There was a coach on the playing field!" Manton charges toward us, motioning at Ash who still kneels next to me, examining my ankle.

I see Butch's bat on the ground. He must've tossed it right behind me when he ran, and that is what I tripped over. That's on me. How could I be so stupid? Still, batters usually don't throw their bats behind the catcher. I mean, if he'd done that on purpose, it would be a real dirty play.

"That was a dead ball! He's not out!" Manton is red-faced and slightly unhinged as he fights against this young umpire's call. You'd think it was the last out of the World Series instead of the first inning of a 14U game. The Blaze are going to kill us anyway. And besides that, Manton is wrong. I caught the ball before Ash or anyone else came out of the dugout. Before I fell, actually.

Ash barely touches my ankle and a pain like I've never experienced before makes me yelp like a little puppy.

"HE'S OUT!" the umpire gives Manton as good as he gets. "He was out before we called time for the injury. Go back over there, Coach! Now! Before I throw you out!"

Manton huffs and puffs and mutters his complaints, but he goes back to the third base box.

My dad is by my side now, and a lot of my Ashafarian teammates gather around, even Julio from way out in right field has come to check on me. The Texas Blaze players are in their dugout, sitting on the bench with their heads hung low. Not a one of them looks at me or anything, but I understand that they can't. They aren't allowed to.

Coach Ash is smiling at me, as if he could care less about anything else going on around the baseball field. "Pete, what did the mitt say to the ball?"

I just look at him.

"Catch you later."

I groan, only partly because of the pain in my ankle.

Ash smiles. "My friend, I think it's time for you to take a trip to the hospital."

19

My mom meets us at the emergency room, and they confirm that the ankle is indeed broken but it is a "minor break" and my tailbone is just bruised but it is a "deep contusion." The doctor recommends that I just keep a temporary splint on the ankle for the evening, and then go to an orthopedic specialist tomorrow morning so he can set it and cast it properly.

They give me some pills for pain and we drive through P.Terry's for a pineapple milkshake. My sister calls me from New York and she makes me laugh, talking about how mom and dad were in a huge panic when they called to tell her what happened.

"We *are* talking about your ankle here, aren't we Peter?" she asks me. "Not exactly a life-threatening injury, am I right?" Her perspective makes me feel a lot better after all the drama of being carried off the field on a volunteer firefighter's gurney while all the players and parents watched.

I tell her that the game announcer had gotten my name wrong as I was carried off, saying, "Let's give a big hand to this very brave young man, Paul Simpson!"

I don't even remember falling asleep, but I wake up in the middle of the night with one thought: I need another pain pill. I slept through the time I was supposed to have a dose, so it is hard to get the pain under control and I can't get comfortable all night. We are waiting at the orthopedist's office when they open the next morning, and they work me in pretty quickly. I choose a neon green color for the cast, and the doctor gives me a waterproof one since it is summer. The good news, according to her, is that the break isn't on my growth plate. She tells me about how to take care of the ankle and all the things I can and can't do.

"When do you think I can play baseball

again?" is my only question.

"Well, there are a lot of variables I need to assess before I can answer that, Pete."

"Well, about how long?"

"I'm not sure..."

"Well, will it be longer than a month? Two months?"

We go back and forth like that for a bit. I guess the doctor doesn't want to give me a definite answer, but she finally sees I need some sort of specific info.

"Okay, Pete, let's say you do everything you're supposed to. Stay off it, take care of yourself, rest and heal. And let's say because you're young and healthy and you mend fast, I can take off the cast in five or six weeks. Then you do all your exercises every day, twice a day, and follow the rehab instructions to the letter... that would be another four weeks. So we're looking at, best case scenario, end of August."

"Baseball season is over by then."

"Let's concentrate on getting you 100% before the first day of high school." She winks.

I hate her a little bit.

Later I check the tournament website. Blaze beat the Ashafarians, 15-2.

By the time I have layed around the house for a couple weeks, my mom and dad are no longer worried about me. Matter of fact, I think they are sick of me. Having them deliver my favorite foods on a tray is replaced by "Why don't you get yourself a bowl of cereal?" I no longer have complete 24-hour jurisdiction over the remote control and we are back to watching my parents' choices: PBS documentaries or the weather unless there is a decent MLB game on. My mom brings a few books home from the library and tells me to pick one and give her an oral report on it by next week. Yeah, that's right. I am home with a broken ankle, no friends, my baseball career is over, it is summer, I haven't heard a word from Livvie or any of my friends, and I have to do a book report.

I choose "Hatchet" by Gary Paulsen because I already read it in school. When I pick it up to flip through, I wind up reading the stupid thing again. It's about this guy around my age who is the only survivor when this private plane crashes, and he has to survive in the wilderness by himself with only a – you guessed it – hatchet. I stay up all night to finish the book even though I know what happens. Whatever, it's pretty decent and it passes the time.

Uncle Luke comes to visit in his vintage pickup truck and brings his tools. He is fixing my chin-up bar. Since that is one of the exercises I can still do, I guess he takes pity on me and decides to come repair it finally. I lie on my bed tossing a baseball in the air over and over while he works.

"So, tell me about your girlfriend," he says with a smile.

"No."

"No, you don't want to tell me?"

"No, I mean I don't have...one."

"What about that girl who plays volleyball, whose brother is on your baseball team?"

"I'm not on that team anymore."

"So she *is* your girlfriend!"

"Think fast." I throw the baseball at him.

He catches it, no problem. "Why don't you call her or something? I could drop you guys at the movies or the mall, or wherever you whippersnappers like to go these days."

Uncle Luke is my mom's much younger brother, and he's not exactly old so it's like a joke when he calls us whippersnappers. He's pretty funny and good to hang around with. Sometimes. But not today.

He tosses the ball back to me. "C'mon. Your cool uncle will take you kids somewhere. What about that arcade place with the restaurant...Sam and Buster's...Ketchup and Mustard's...Phil and Lester's? My treat."

"Not happening." I start tossing the ball up in the air again. Up, catch. Up, catch. Up, catch.

"Yeah, I can see you'd have a lot more fun here, doing that."

"Less talk, more work over there," I tell him.

"Yes sir."

He gets the chin up bar re-attached. "That oughta work. Try it out."

I hobble over to test it. It is solid, and I lift myself a few times. Chin-ups are pretty hard.

"You know, there are crazy people in all walks of life, right?" Luke watches me graze my chin on the bar. "I mean we all have to deal with it. Take this guy I know at work, okay? He wears a white turtleneck. Ev-er-y day. A white turtleneck And wait for it...he tucks it in."

I have to laugh which makes me stop with the pull-ups. I lean in the doorway and listen to my uncle.

"And he's a nutcase for other reasons too – I mean, as if the turtlenecks weren't enough. This guy, he thinks he's amazing, he has this grandiose sense of his own importance. And he doesn't care about anyone else or if he gets them in trouble or anything – absolutely no remorse. You know that the average person is four times more likely to have a psychopath for a boss than to be the manager of a psychopath, right?"

"What are you talking about?" I am definitely laughing now.

"I'm trying to tell you kid, there are crazy people everywhere. This Coach Manton won't be your last nutcase."

I kind of stop laughing at that. "Whatever," I say. "I mean, you don't really know him."

"Okay, okay. I'm sure he has his good side and all that. Everybody does. But I just want you to remember one thing."

I hop back to   the bed and put

my cast up on a pillow. It is hurting.

"Are you listening?" Uncle Luke asks me.

I am, sort of.

"Just remember this, Pete. It's not you, it's him."

"I know that," I say.

"Do you?"

After Uncle Luke leaves, I think over what he said. He's kind of right, but he doesn't know Coach Manton like I do. He loves baseball. And Coach wants the best for us in the long run, he just has to do what's necessary to get us there sometime. People who aren't on the team don't understand.

"Lakers have their first game today!" my dad tells me one afternoon.

I was kind of dozing off but I open my eyes. "So?"

"So you're one of the coaches!" His enthusiasm is not infectious.

"I don't think I'd be much help."

"Of course you would! You have crutches, you can get around. It's not like you have to play, you'll just be coaching. Teaching them how to do it does not involve doing it yourself."

"It sort of does," I tell him.

"Be ready at three, I'll drive you over."

Even Dad is being strict now. What have I done to deserve this? Excuse me for breaking my ankle.

My phone buzzes and, just like every time I get a text or a call these days, I hope it is Livvie. I'm absolutely sure she has heard about my ankle by now, but she's never contacted me. Of course, I haven't contacted her either. But I am the one who was hurt.

It isn't Livvie, just Coach Ash. He has been checking in every day, usually with some stupid joke. Today's is: *Why did Cinderella get kicked off the baseball team?*

I really don't want to text him back. I wish he'd just leave me alone. Baseball is over for me. Done. Finito. Goodbye.

Another text from him: *You know you want to know the answer...*

I bite. I mean if I don't reply, he'll probably just keep bothering me. *Ok, why?*

Cinderella got kicked off the baseball team because she ran away from the ball.

I don't want to encourage him so I don't reply.

I look back through my old texts and see that video link Ash sent awhile back. I could never get it to download but I decide to try again and it works. Probably another one of Ash's very lame attempts at humor.

It's some grainy footage of a basketball game, looks like a few decades ago. A title comes up: "Indiana University practice, 1997, Bobby Knight. " The white-haired coach in his red pullover sweater walks up to a player in the middle of the court, obviously yelling. It gives me a weird feeling in the pit of my stomach. The coach grabs the player around the neck with his right hand and seems to start choking him. The player walks backward, trying to get away. The video switches to another title: "Rutgers University practice, 2011, Mike Rice." This coach pushes, screams curses, grabs jerseys, throws balls at players. And then it switches to another coach, another practice. Throwing chairs. Grabbing players. Pushing, shoving. It's a montage of tons of different crazy coaches over the years, all of them losing it.

I realize I'm sweating. My hands are shaking. It is like I am watching history repeat itself, over and over.

What is Ash trying to say here? That this sort of behavior is common and we should just put up with it?

At the end of the video, some words crawl across the screen: *Coach abuse is a widespread problem in our society today. Do you know a youth coach who values winning over the player's wellbeing? Coaches who put victory above the welfare of young athletes--*

I delete the video from my phone. I don't want to see any more. What's the point?

20

Someone has actually mown the grass at the Little League field. Arnie has chalked out some lines and Zach has gotten somebody to donate gimme caps and yellow t-shirts printed with the word LAKERS in purple. We now have enough real baseball gloves to field nine players at once.

Hey, we are a team.

The boys are beyond excited, bouncing around in the dugout and everybody asking if they can bat first. To keep them busy, I find a marker and let them take turns signing my cast.

Lots of parents and neighbors and kids

and dogs and friends have come out. I'm kind of surprised at all the activity, considering this was basically an abandoned field not too long ago. We are playing West Austin today, with their striped pants and fitted caps and matching equipment bags. An older guy pushes an ice cream cart by the field, chanting "Paletas... Popsicles... Helado... Ice Cream..." I see one of the moms from West Austin who won't let her little kid buy any, telling him, "That's yucky, we'll go to Pinkberry later."

The game is a comedy of errors, and I stress errors. Neither team is entirely clear on the rules and the coaches spend their time shouting basic handy tips like "run!" and "throw it!" I am elected to be the third base coach even though I'm on crutches. Theo plays catcher and I have to say, he is one of the best players out there.

At one point in between innings, he asks if he can keep my catcher's gear for his own and take it home with him. Of course I say yes. I mean, I sure don't need it anymore. And to tell you the truth, I'm sort of touched. That is, until Theo tells me it's because he wants to wear the catcher's gear for Halloween next fall, since he's going to be a Teenage Mutant Ninja Turtle. He's going to wear the chest plate on his back, and maybe paint it green. It does look a little like a turtle shell, now that I think about it. I tell him to save a couple of Reese's for me and he says, no way – but he'll give me all the Almond Joys.

My mom walks over from the library when she is done with work, and she gets to see the Lakers score their only two runs. She and my dad are cheering like crazy, and I have to admit – so am I.

After the game, Theo's sister gives all the boys water out of a big jug she's brought from home. I have $20 burning a hole in my pocket, since Uncle Luke gave it to me and said, "Show your girlfriend a good time, why don't ya?" Like that's going to happen. So I flag down the ice cream cart and get one for every kid on the team, plus Arnie and Zach. Zach says a little prayer of thanks for this wonderful day and the difference God is making in these young boys' lives. When it's time to go, Theo makes me bend down so he can give me a slap on the cheek.

All the heat and sweat of the Little League game makes me realize that it is really true what people say about casts – they are uncomfortable and they itch. My mom suggests they drop me off at the pool for a dip, and they'll come pick me up later. My mom and dad exchange some sort of meaningful glance, and my dad adds, "Swimming is great exercise, especially while you're laid up like this."

Okay, whatever. I'll go. Maybe today is the day there will finally be someone working at the guard gate who will bust me as a non-member of the Cedar Hills Club. Even though I'm on crutches, they'll kick me out on the street. That's probably the next step in my total ostracism.

We pull up to the pool, there aren't many cars in the parking lot which is a good sign. As my folks are driving away and I am hobbling through the pool gate, I see what that look between my parents must've been about.

The lifeguard is Livvie.

I remember the clue she gave me about her maybe summer job: she held her nose.

Like she was underwater.

I stop just inside the gate, ready to turn around and leave. I don't have my phone. My mom suggested I leave it with her, "so it doesn't get wet." I am beginning to feel trapped here, and like this was all a set-up.

Livvie looks right at me. Even with her

zinc oxide nose, dark sunglasses and Texas Blaze baseball cap, I can see she is surprised. She sits atop the tall lifeguard stand, wearing a white tank top with a big red cross on the front. She looks at me for no more than two seconds, then goes back to scanning the pool.

Little kids splash and scream. A silver-haired man swims laps, slow and steady. A few dads sit on lounge chairs with no sunscreen on their pale chests, each immersed in their own cell phone. The moms with toddlers huddle together in the shallow end, solving the problems of the world and of the local elementary school.

I walk all the way around the pool, as far from Livvie's lifeguard perch as I can get. I find a chair and ease into it, only to realize that where I sit is directly in Livvie's sight line. Dang it. It's like I am purposely trying to be seen by her – and nothing could be further from the truth.

I kick off my one sneaker and peel my t-shirt, then hop across the warm pavement and fall into the pool. The cold water is a jolt, but it quickly feels fantastic. The coolness oozes inside my cast, relieving the itch. To get back to the surface, I have to kick double hard since I can only use one leg plus I am pulling up the extra heaviness of the cast. I break into air and grab onto the side, not used to swimming in the deep end with this weight around my ankle. I glance at Livvie without meaning to, and see her staring right at me. She probably thinks I am drowning or something. This just gets worse and worse.

Livvie lifts the whistle around her neck and blasts it. "No running!"

Some little boys who are chasing their Frisbee downshift into a speed walk. I wonder how many times a day the average lifeguard has to tell someone not to run. At least twenty or thirty, I'm willing to bet.

I make a pact with myself not to look in Livvie's direction again. I experiment with a couple of different strokes, but don't get too far. I can't float either with this cast pulling me down. I settle on just staying submerged up to my neck while I hang on to the side of the pool. The water feels too good to get out. I close my eyes and try to relax... just feeling the waves and listening to kids yelling Marco Polo while the parents gossip.

"Hey." Livvie is squatting right next to me. "Are you okay?"

"Why? Do I look like I'm drowning?"

"I'm on break, so if you are he'll have to help you."

The lifeguard up on the chair now is a guy in high school that I've seen around, a football player. He's definitely been lifting weights this summer.

"I think I'm fine."

Livvie smiles a little and sits down criss-cross applesauce, as my sister always calls it. "How's the ankle?" she says.

"Okay. How's the job?"

"Good."

I pull myself up out of the water and perch on the edge next to her.

"Let me see that." She points to my cast and I swing it up on the side.

"Theo, age 6," she reads the scrawled signatures. "Jaxon, 5 years old. Your new friends seem to be obsessed with their ages."

"It's community service."

"You broke the law?"

"Noooo."

"Oh, you mean they did? Theo, age 6, convicted felon."

"It's a Little League team, I'm just helping out. They needed assistant coaches."

Livvie's real smile shines through for the first time today.

"It was my mom's idea," I add.

"You, a coach. I love it."

"Well, don't get too used to the idea."

"No, seriously. I can see you all grown up, coaching a kids' baseball team or something."

"Yeah, since I'll never make it in the Major Leagues. Or even the high school team."

"I didn't say that. But everybody has to retire eventually."

"Yeah, I guess you're right." I go along with the idea. "Eventually you have to grow up, settle down, start a family."

"Okay, now you're freaking me out a little," she says and she's not entirely joking.

"So how're the Blaze doing?"

She takes a deep breath. "Well, they did have a losing record for the season if you can believe that, but this weekend they won three games and made it to the finals – where they lost. But that at least pulled them above .500. Just barely. It's still their worst season ever, obvi."

I'm not proud of the fact that this makes me a little happy.

"So all the parents are, like, freaking out," she continues. "Mr. Loezier got this university batting coach to come analyze everyone's swings on a computer or something. It's kind of crazy.. Especially since all they need is a good catcher. Know any?"

"How's soccer?"

"Good, but volleyball's better. We won the Under Armour Invitational in Dallas!" Her eyes light up. "In the 15U division! These girls were in high school, and I swear to you, there were girls that were, like, six foot three. I'm not even kidding. They spike it like, bloop! Easy. But believe it or not, Sasha got tourney MVP – and I could hardly lift her trophy. It was huge. It was awesome. We went to Six Flags on the way home and it was... it was really fun."

I submerge my cast back in the water and feel it pulling me down. "That's cool."

I hear them before I see them. Bellows and Butch and Louie come barreling through the gate running and playing chase, like they own the place. When they get to the edge of the pool, Louie manages to push in both Bellows and Butch while they are still in their flip-flops and sunglasses. The waves almost topple a baby wearing floaties. When Butch and Bellows come up for air, a few choice words are exchanged between them and Louie. Moms cover their toddlers' ears.

"Hey, you guys! Cut it out!" Livvie shouts. "Maniacs," she mutters under her breath.

When they look at Livvie, they see me. It is only a matter of time until they make their way to this part of the pool. Or else they are going to ignore me, which might be worse.

"Well, I guess my break's about over," Livvie says as the other lifeguard motions her over.

"Okay. See ya." I don't even look up. Her feet stand next to me, maybe waiting for me to look up or maybe she's busy watching the guys mess around in the pool.

"Okay then," she says.

"Pete!" It's Alicia Caldwell. I hadn't even noticed her, or maybe she just got here.

"How aaaaaaare you?" she asks me.

Even though Alicia talks in that fake popular-girl voice, like she's so excited to see everyone, I think she is actually an okay person. I mean, she's not as bad as some people think she is. We were lab partners in 6th grade and she's totally regular under all that...that everything.

I see Louie and the guys notice that Alicia has bent over to hug me. Livvie still stands next to me, even though I thought her break was over.

"Hey Alicia, what's up?" I say.

She takes this as an invitation to sit down next to me. "Hi Livvie. Listen, Pete, I wanted to say – it was soooooo nice talking to you on the phone that night!"

"Um..."

I turn toward Livvie but she just gives me a quick smile and heads toward the lifeguard stand. Alicia leans into me and speaks in a less public voice.

"Remember, when the guys called me? To give me a hard time about Richard and all that? You were, like, the only one who was normal to me that night."

"Oh, yeah."

Never have I been happier to see the old Prius pull up.

"Anyway, thanks for that," she says.

"No problem."

"Pete, can I ask you something? Does Richard have a girlfriend at St. Anthony's? Do you know?"

"No, I don't think so. But uh, I have to go. I'll see you later." I try to stand on one foot.

Alicia gets up and hands me my crutches. "Hope your foot gets all better soon."

"Thanks. Me too."

I fumble with the crutches as I gather my stuff. Alicia stretches out on a lounge chair like she's modeling for an advertisement. I make my way carefully across the wet pavement, dropping my towel along the way. Livvie trots over and picks it up, I guess in her official lifeguard capacity.

"I got it," I tell her.

"Pete?"

"Yeah?"

Livvie's words come tumbling out, barely above a whisper. "Listen, Coach Manton is going in front of the school board next week, for approval." She glances over her shoulder at Louie and Butch, but they are busy splashing Alicia.

"They do it for all the new hires," she continues. "You know they vote on them and stuff. A bunch of the guys are going – I mean they are going to support him and all that, but it's just – well, you know. I just... wanted you to know."

"Okaaaay..." I say.

She opens the gate for me.

"Well, people are going to stand up in front of the school board and talk about Manton, so..."

Richard walks in the gate and we're all sort of surprised to see each other.

"Pete! What are you doing..." He catches himself. "I mean, hi."

"Hey Richard. I've been meaning to return those swim trunks you lent me. I'm not stealing them or anything-"

"Don't worry about it, man. I've been wanting to call you – "

I really do not want to hear Richard Loezier's words of pity right now.

"I'll leave 'em on your porch! Bye. Bye, Livvie." I hustle into the Prius and slam the door. I turn to talk to my dad, ignoring Richard and Livvie.

21

The doctor is really happy with my progress, and I wind up getting my cast off even though it's only been four and a half weeks. Only! Seems like forever. Anyway, I'm happy to be done with it and I start doing the gentle foot rotations and other exercises and stretches just like she says. I do the ice and the heat and I even use arnica cream, which is some herbal remedy that my mom swears by. It can't hurt.

Why I am in such a hurry to rehab this ankle, I'm not sure. But I don't let myself think about that.

One day I wake up feeling so good, I think

I can actually take a little batting practice. My dad goes with me to the cages and helps me carry my equipment over. Then he finds a place in the shade to sit and play on his phone. Dear old Dad has finally discovered Words With Friends. For him, this is the cutting edge of technology. Anyway, he's officially an addict now. He has about fifty games going at once, with everyone he knows. Mom calls him GameBoy. I tried to explain that a GameBoy is a handheld device and that doesn't make sense as a nickname – but she won't stop.

I go slow as I unpack my bat and helmet, no hurry. I stretch and warm up with care. My only thought is getting the full range of motion, having a healthy ankle once again. Baseball is such an ingrained habit, I just want to know I can still hit, even if it's in the cage.

I set up the tee and get in position. I wind up and – *whoosh.* I miss the ball completely.

I can't even hit the ball off the tee? What the hell?

"Pete!" Richard is walking up from the parking lot. Looks like his mom just dropped him off. I guess he has the same idea as me, to get in a little BP.

"Richard, hey."

I put another ball on the tee, and this time I hit it.

Richard and I both act like there's nothing unusual, we are just doing our own thing, hitting and practicing like we are still two guys on the same team. He asks if I want to take turns throwing some soft toss, so we pitch to each other from behind a screen inside one of the cages. Richard's swing is looking really sharp and I say as much. He pitches to me for a long time, even though I say that's enough. He keeps on going. My ankle is surprisingly good, just a little tight but no pain. I don't want to overdo it so I finally go to put my bat away.

"Thanks, man," I tell Richard.

"Anytime. You should just call whenever you come down here, I'll meet you."

"I don't know how often that will be now." I try to laugh but it doesn't come out right.

I'm zipping up my bag when Richard squats down next to me. "Pete? Listen..."

"You don't have to say anything."

"No, it's not that. Listen... I already talked to my dad and everything. Actually, it was my dad's idea."

What is Mr. Loezier's idea? This doesn't sound good. I stand up to take weight off my ankle.

"Pete, we could really use you at St. Anthony's. I mean, on the baseball team, and at the school and everything."

"What?"

I'm totally caught off guard. St. Anthony's? That is the super nice private school where Richard goes. He starts babbling about me starting there in the fall.

"That's nice and all," I tell him. "But I don't think so. I mean, thanks though." I pick up my bag.

"Wait, listen – it's a scholarship thing. A full scholarship. My dad already talked to them and he's going to be calling your parents. It's all official. I'm not supposed to say anything probably, but they are going to be contacting you. I just wanted to give you a heads up. And tell you that I...think it would be cool."

"Are you saying it's a baseball scholarship to St Anthony's?"

"Yeah, baseball and academics. You've got the grades and everything. You are, like, exactly what they are always saying they want over there – the scholar-athlete and all of that."

I am exactly what they want at St. Anthony's? Come on. This is ridiculous. I have really become the charity case now.

"Am I being punk'd or something? Where are the hidden cameras?" I ask.

Richard relaxes a little, relieved that I finally smiled. "Look, I know this might seem a little weird. Unexpected. But just think about it. It would be so great, you know, for me. To have a friend on the team."

Richard looks down, that shy side of his coming through. The thought of Richard not having friends at St. Anthony's has never occurred to me. I figured he was the big shot over there with all his rich friends.

"There are lots of scholarship kids, over half the people at the school are on some kind of financial aid or whatever. And no one knows who is who, they don't allow you to say if you're on scholarship or not. Except for me, of course. Everybody definitely knows I didn't get in for brains or athletic skill." He smiles.

Richard sounds like he wishes he could

be a scholarship student.

"Luckily I have good ol' Mr. Loezier to pay my way," he adds. We both break into a laugh.

"I should go," I tell him.

"Just think about it."

"Yeah, okay, I guess. And listen, Richard, you know – you should call Alicia sometime."

That afternoon, I tell my parents I want to take a walk, to help rehab my ankle. They barely notice as I leave because they are so engrossed in some conversation about a documentary on a Chinese artist who was arrested in his country for criticizing the government. You see the sort of boring stuff I have to listen to?

I take it slow and wind up around on the backside of the baseball field, where there are trees. You can walk up from that direction and not be noticed as much. In some part of my brain, I knew I was coming here. Another part of me feels surprised to be watching the Texas Blaze practice from this side of the fence.

I find a spot in the crook of a tree and pull myself up to sit. I'm out of sight there so I can watch without being seen, and it also feels good to rest my ankle. I had to walk a couple of miles to get here and it's throbbing a little.

The practice is just like many I've been to over the years. The drills and exercises are like second nature to me. I see Butch and Louie laughing at something. I bite my lip, trying not to think how I won't ever be a part of this again.

It's toward the end of practice, during game situations, that Coach starts to lose it. Watching from here, I get a different perspective. I can almost understand why he is so frustrated. Dropped balls and mistakes look so different from this side of the fence – why don't they just catch it? It's like Manton knows exactly where he wants each player to go and exactly what he wants each of them to do, but when they don't fulfill that, his frustration level rises.

Did you ever have one of those little plastic disc toys that was a maze with a little metal BB inside? And you try and get that BB to go this way and that, but it never does what you want? It will never land in the clown's nose or whatever? I think that's how Coach feels – he has this idea of baseball perfection in his mind, but I guess real life is not always like that.

Manton yells and fumes and frets at Richard and Louie and Butch and the new catcher. Especially the new catcher, who looks a little lost. I hate to say that, considering that's my old position, but tonight it is kind of true. The kid looks like he'd rather be back on the Twisters – or anywhere – but here.

I pull out my phone and switch the camera to video. It feels like I am just now deciding to do this, but I realize that's not entirely true. Why did I sneak over here? Why did I climb into this tree so I'd have a clear vantage point? Hands shaking, I point the camera at Manton and push record.

It doesn't take too long before Coach loses it. I think maybe Louie said something just then under his breath – I'm not sure, but whatever just happened definitely sets off Manton. He starts screaming and cussing and he pushes the new catcher quite hard. Although I'm not sure of exactly the situation, I know that kid probably didn't talk back or anything. But I also know that bullies sometimes like to pick on the weak.

Maybe it's just because I'm seeing it through a camera that Coach's behavior seems worse than usual. After all, isn't this what was happening at almost every practice by the time I quit? Still, it seems really harsh when I know it's being recorded. At one point, Manton picks up a baseball and pegs Butch right in the arm. Butch squeals involuntarily and holds his arm, but quickly pretends it doesn't hurt.

I notice some movement in the trees near me. I click off my camera and hold my breath, not wanting to be seen. Not that they could prove I was doing anything wrong – not that I was doing anything wrong, but it would feel sort of awkward for someone to find me up here watching the Blaze practice. It's like I'm spying or something. And I guess I am.

I try to see who it is, but I can't make them out. The lights have switched on illuminating the field, making this stand of trees seem even darker. The person coughs and when they turn their head, I get a glimpse. It takes me a minute, but I realize who it is.

That mean old man who glared at me when I got thrown out at third.

I realize I have seen this man other times too, with his beat-up Texas Blaze hat, stalking behind the stands at our games. I've caught glimpses of him here and there at different games. I never saw him enough to even wonder who he was. Until now. What's he doing hiding over here, watching the practice?

I guess he would ask the same about me.

Coach Manton is still furious, screaming at the catcher again now. He puts his catcher's mask back on, probably to cover tears of frustration that are filling his eyes. I know that trick well.

I pull my phone out again and press record, a little bit afraid of what I might be about to film.

22

My mom finds out that poor kids (or as she calls them, "underserved populations") can get discounted tickets to see Round Rock Express games. She decides Theo and his friends should go.

The Express are part of the professional Triple A Minor League, and have a stadium in a suburb north of Austin. They are a really good team and have guys called up regularly to the Rangers. I've been to their games before and it's a lot of fun, but to tell you the truth I don't really feel like going now. Still, my mom applied for these discounted tickets weeks ago, and she actually winds up getting 15 tickets for free. Enough for all the Lakers and their coaches. Arnie and Zach borrow a van from their church or something and before you can say "No thanks, I'd rather stay home and play xBox," we are taking the Lakers to see a professional baseball game.

What these kids lack in knowledge about baseball, they definitely make up for in enthusiasm. And not only are they excited about the thrill of the game and the beauty of the sport, they also love the sno-cones. Dell Diamond has a bouncy castle and a playscape and a twisty slide and a swimming pool. And a big grassy area to run around. Yeah, this is a kid's dream place, no doubt about it.

Since the boys are running every which direction, we decide that Arnie, Zach and I will each take four kids. I get Theo and three of his buddies. After some junk food, they each take ten turns on the slide and then we do a thorough tour of the gift shop even though we're not buying anything. Finally, we settle in to actually watch some baseball. I'm telling them a little about the game, and they actually seem to be getting it.

"He was out!" one of the kids says about a play at second base.

"No, he had to tag him because that

wasn't a force out," Theo gravely explains.

For some dumb reason, I feel like my heart will about burst.

It's just kind of gratifying that Theo understands what a force out at second is. I mean, just a couple of months ago Theo didn't know anything about baseball. I feel like he has actually been listening to some of the stuff I've told him. And right then, Theo leans over and puts his head against me. He probably has a tummy ache from all the junk food or something, so I just put my arm around him and we watch the game.

Arnie and Zach find their way over to where we are sitting and all twelve of the boys are enjoying the game. I am too, actually. Okay Mom, you were right – it was a good idea to come. Hate when that happens.

I notice a couple of men about ten rows down. Something about them keeps catching my eye. I don't know why, but I can't help glancing down there in between every pitch. One of them is hunched down in his seat and they both wear baseball caps... It takes a minute, but I finally realize it is Coach Manton. And that old man.

My first thought is to get up and leave,

but of course I can't. I decide to just not draw attention to myself, look the other way and ignore them. They'll never notice me. And even if they did, I'm certain they wouldn't acknowledge me. Still, just their presence is ruining the game for me.

For some reason, I can't keep my eyes from straying ten rows down. The two of them sit mostly in silence, watching the game, but the old man periodically lectures Manton on what various players are doing incorrectly. I can make out snippets of the usual sort of know-it-all complaining you can hear in any ballpark: "What he should've done right there was run over and step on second before he threw it..." or "See, his problem is mechanics, he turns his hips *too* much when he swings..."

Everyone's an expert in the stands.

Even me, come to think of it.

The more I listen to the old man's comments, the more I realize that they sound just like Coach Manton. It hits me: This older man must be his father, because his words and his mannerisms – and most importantly, his opinions on baseball – sound just like Coach. Strangely, Manton barely says anything but just slumps in his seat and listens.

Sort of like a moody adolescent.

Theo feels heavy against my side and I realize he's falling asleep. All the kids are getting fidgety or very, very still – either way, it means they are tired. Arnie says we need to go soon and we start telling the kids to gather their trash and put their sneakers back on. (Yes, most of them took off their shoes. Don't ask). I'm busy tying a shoelace when I hear that old man's voice getting closer.

"He has to extend, he's never going to get any velocity with a step-out extension like that..."

They are walking up the steps, soon to pass right by me. I keep my head down.

Coach Manton decides to interject a bit into the old man's diatribe. "Dad, it was a fly ball right to the center fielder. That is a good pitch, by any standards, especially at this level of play –"

Manton's father says, "Are you talking back to me? *That's it!*"

I look up just as the old man kind of cuffs Manton in the chest, throwing him off balance a little.

Manton just says, "Dad," in a sort of tired

239

voice.

"*What did you say?*" the old man snarls and stops, going nose to nose with Manton in a menacing way.

It's like déjà vu. Manton and his dad speak – and act – just alike.

"WATCH OUT!" Zach yells.

Everyone turns to look, even Manton and his dad. I look up to see a homerun ball heading right for us. On instinct, I take off the baseball cap I'm wearing and catch the ball right inside the hat. It had been headed towards a sleepy Theo, so it was kind of lucky I caught it.

"Nice one!" says Arnie.

"Lemme see it!" says Theo, who is now wide awake.

As the boys gather around to see the real, live MLB baseball, I glance up. Manton is standing just a few feet away, staring right at me.

I remember how the first time Coach ever saw me was when I caught that ball in my hat during 6th grade tryouts.

That was a long time ago.

"Hi, Coach."

23

I come clean to my parents about eve-rything. I mean, not about sneaking out to meet Livvie in the middle of the night – but I tell them all the details about how Coach Manton kneed me in the chest and how he lifted Louie up and banged him against the wall and then he pushed me down in the dugout and I hit my head. That takes "getting benched" to a whole new level, my dad says. Even my mom laughs, but I think she's wiping away a couple of tears too.

Listing all the things that happened, and answering my mom's questions ("Were you scared?" Well, duh.) makes me realize that it has been a pretty bad situation. Okay, a really bad situation.

The more the Blaze lost, the more Manton lost it. At unpredictable times and for very small reasons. Like when I saw him the other night at the Express game, my heart started doing its rat-a-tat-tat rhythm and I was thinking crazy things like, "where is the closest security guard" and "if I have to, I will move away from Theo so he won't have to witness Coach Manton's freak out." It's unbelievable that a man who inspires that sort of panic is allowed to coach youth sports, am I right?

But yet, it's Coach Manton. I mean, he's not like pure evil or anything. There's a part of me – a big part of me – that still really respects him. He knows so much about baseball, and he really did mold the Texas Blaze into one of the best 14U teams in Central Texas. Not to brag or anything, but he taught us a lot. And if he hadn't put me on the team and believed in me when no one else did, where would I be now?

I also know I have actually been living in fear for awhile now – everyone on the team has, although I'm not sure Louie or Butch will ever admit that. But I saw the look in

Louie's eyes when Manton was shaking him. He was scared. We were all scared, whether anyone wants to own up to it or not.

I kind of break down and my mom puts her arms around me and then my dad comes over, too. There we are at the kitchen table, in a group hug, stuck together in this knowledge that the world is not perfect.

"I have an itch on my back, can somebody scratch it?" says Dad.

"My foot's asleep," says Mom.

It's never felt better to laugh. I think keeping a secret has been this tiny little pressure inside my brain – and now it's released. I feel like I just walked out of a math test. I may not get an A, but at least it's over.

I have this very rudimentary editing app on my laptop. It is ridiculously complicated, but it does the job. With all the videos I download off my phone, I create a sort of "greatest hits" of the yelling and screaming and pushing that Manton did at the practice where I climbed in the tree and taped him. I slow it down in parts and even repeat certain physical pushes and shoves. For a second I think I'm sensationalizing it, but then I sit up straight and take a deep breath. Manton did these things, and he should see them.

Before I have a chance to wuss out, I press SEND. The video has gone to Manton's email address.

You know how people say they have butterflies in their stomach? Well I have more like hungry velociraptors. Who are fighting.

I feel I've crossed a line and I can't go back.

This is not good. Manton is going to freak.

24

The school board meeting is packed. Apparently there's a lot of fascinating stuff on the agenda (not) and approving the new baseball coach is way down the list, scheduled toward the end. First, the curriculum director is going to lull us all to sleep with a power point comparing two different U.S. history textbooks. My mom actually winds up raising her hand and commenting on one of the textbooks, calling it "partisan misinformation."

What is she doing? My dad quietly reminds her why we're here.

We sit on one side of the room along with

Uncle Luke, who happened to be in town, and my sister who's home visiting. They both came to the meeting even though I told them not to. My sister said she wouldn't miss it. Uncle Luke said he didn't have anything better to do.

With all of us there, the Simmons family takes up half a row. Across the room is the entire Texas Blaze team – Louie and Butch and Richard and Bellows and Flat-Top and everybody. Livvie sits in the middle of all the guys and mostly seems to be looking down at her phone. I'm not sure what Richard is doing here, since he doesn't attend Welton, but I guess the whole team decided to come support Coach.

Butch wears a tie. I'd bet a hundred bucks Butch's dad made him wear the tie, but he looks good actually. All the Blaze parents are here, and my mom and dad wave to a couple of them. Mr. Loezier gives my dad a big greeting. They've been talking on the phone a lot about that scholarship offer for me, but I don't think I'm going to take it after all. My mother is a big proponent of public education. Also, she heard they haze freshman at St. Anthony's and the faculty just looks the other way and lets it happen. I am sort of glad Mom doesn't like the idea of me going to private school, because no matter what else they do have at St. Anthony's, I know they don't have Livvie. Not that I'm planning my whole life around a girl or anything, but I just want to stay at Welton no matter what happens. I can still play baseball in the summers with Ash.

Manton's crazy father is here, looking like your average proud, nice old man. He's wearing a flannel shirt, even though it's 104 outside, which is kind of weird. But other than that, he seems normal. At one point, he even stands up and gives a woman his seat like a gentleman should. I'm all the sudden worrying that I got this all wrong... He can't be the crazy person I saw at the Express game.

I shake off that idea like a bad pitch sign.

Coach Manton sits alone, at the end of the back row. Maybe he just wants to be on the aisle so he can get up and speak. Maybe he is back there in case he wants to make a quick exit. In any case, he doesn't smile or speak to anyone. He never looks my way, but I don't want to read anything in to that. He probably just doesn't see me.

Finally, the school board gets around to the new baseball coach position. The superintendent reads Manton's list of qualifications out loud. He graduated from some college with a long name like Wichita Polytechnic Agricultural Institute of something or other. Then he played a year of semi-pro for the San Luis Obispo Blues. What they don't mention is the reason his baseball playing career ended, which is a giant scar across his left kneecap. When we were in sixth grade, Coach Manton told us about all the surgeries he had on that knee. During one of them, he was awake when they did it and the doctor had his gloved hand inside Manton's kneecap feeling around for some floating bone chips, but he couldn't find any... So Manton puts on a rubber glove and reached in there himself. We all sort of thought that it couldn't be true, but then again maybe it was. Anyway, the school superintendent doesn't talk about Manton's career-ending knee injury at the age of 22.

Next Butch's dad gets up and talks about what a great and devoted youth coach Manton is and blah, blah, blah. Then some player who now plays baseball at OU stands and gives this heartfelt little speech about how Manton made him a man. At one point in the middle of that long glowing talk, I glance over and Manton actually smiles at me... As if to say, "Top that!"

He's calling my bluff.

I can feel my heart pounding in my ears. It is now or never.

And...I'm thinking never.

Yeah, never sounds good.

I keep quiet. I feel my sister shift in her seat. Livvie is examining a button on her shirt. Dad clears his throat. Manton is smiling and nodding to some people sitting around him. I see him reach inside his wallet and pull out a crumpled piece of yellow paper. It sort of reminds me of the thing that blew out of his wallet that time, when Coach chased it a half mile down the street.

Things are coming to a vote. "All in favor of approving this hiring decision for the new varsity baseball coach position of Welton High School..."

I stand and say that I have signed up to speak. The whole room turns to look at me. The superintendent seems surprised, but she looks over the list and sees that I am on it, so she nods and I walk to the front of the room.

I am careful not to look at Livvie. I don't want to know what she is thinking right now. I have been imagining that when I talked to her at the pool that   day, she was encouraging me to come to this meeting, but maybe she had been warning me off it. Either way, it is too late to change now.

Someone's cell phone rings – and it is a profane rap song. Most of the people in the room laugh. I see Bellows reach for his phone, face turning bright red.

It takes me a minute, opening my backpack and fumbling with the cords I have brought, but I hook my laptop to this white board overhead projector. I say my name and say that I played for three years for Coach Manton and –

"Excuse me, ma'am, sir, excuse me – but what does this have to do with anything? This is just a kid!" It is Manton's father addressing the school board.

The superintendent explains that I have a right to speak and Old Man Manton sits down in a bit of a huff, complaining under his breath to no one in particular.

I am losing my nerve, so I just ask if I can share a video. There are rumblings of discontent and I see Coach Manton shift in his seat.

"It's only about a one minute video, but I think it's...kind of...important?" My voice goes high and I sound incredibly unsure.

I see my dad nodding and smiling. So are my mom and my sister and my uncle. Now I'm glad they came.

"That will be fine, but your time is almost up," the superintendent says. She's shuffling through papers, already mentally engaged in the meeting's next agenda item.

I get the screen to light up, and now visible is a picture of Manton at that practice, with the big white PLAY triangle in the center. I hover the cursor over that triangle, about to start the video, when Coach Manton stands up.

"Stop it or *that's it!*" he yells.

The school board members snap their heads in attention, along with everyone else in the room.

"You hear me, turn that thing off!" He starts to walk toward me, in that menacing way which is all too familiar.

My Blaze teammates kind of realize what's happening. They whisper and poke each other, eyes wide.

"Play it!" one of the guys sings out in a falsetto. Hard to tell which, but it sounds kind of like Butch.

Coach Manton turns to the school board. "I apologize, let me explain. This boy here –" He waves dismissively toward me, "— was a player on my select team who, unfortunately, I had to let go, because he was a problem –"

"ExcUUUUUUUSE me?!" My mother can have a bit of an attitude when she wants to. I once saw her ream this guy who cut in line in front of a pregnant woman. It wasn't pretty.

"Okay, order, order!" The superintendent is clearly confused by the sudden commotion. "Mr. Manton, please sit down. Ma'am, please."

My mother watches as Coach takes a seat, on the front row now.

"Now, uh –" The superintendent consults her papers. "Pete Simons?"

"Simmons," I tell her.

"Do you want to share something?"

The room is still. I consider turning around and walking away. Going to St. Anthony's. Moving back to East Austin. Anything but this.

"Yes, ma'am. I do."

"Then please, go ahead. Sometime in this century, if you don't mind."

I reach for the mouse and that's when Manton springs out of his seat.

"What? You think you know me? You think because you recorded one little moment – completely out of context – that you know what I am about as a coach? You know nothing!"

"Mr. Manton, please!" says the superintendent.

People all around the room are wide-eyed, mouths hanging open.

"I worked for 25 years coaching baseball teams, to get this chance! I have put in the blood, sweat and tears – and I deserve this position! You think you know about me? You know nothing!"

"I know one thing," I tell Coach Manton, as calmly as I can muster. "The way you treat us is probably exactly the way your dad treated you. But that doesn't make it right. The cycle has got to end sometime."

I see different emotions flicker across his face. Surprise. Embarrassment. Disbelief. And finally, a building fury.

"What is that supposed to mean?" yells the old man. "I made you what you are!"

"Well, that's true," I say.

"Don't let him disrespect you like that!" Manton's dad stands up, red-faced. I swear, he is exactly like his son. Or vice versa.

I move my finger to press play, and that's when Manton pushes me. I fall back into the seats behind me. There is gasping and screaming. The superintendent bangs her gavel. A security guard runs into the room.

The video I made begins to play: *For your consideration as the next coach of the varsity baseball team at Welton High School, please meet Mr. Ashland Keele.* After that first still photo of Coach Manton, the rest of the video is a little mini biography of Ash I put together, highlighting his stellar career as a scholar athlete, from high school to the Ivy League and then two years with Teach for America. As I made this video, I realized Ash was even more highly qualified than I'd thought. I even did a little interview with him, where Ash talks about his "win-some-lose-some" philosophy and how you have to understand the rhythms of baseball and learn to gracefully accept defeat in order to be mentally ready for the next victory.

Of course, no one is watching the video. A few men are busy escorting Manton out of the building. Most everyone else is buzzing with shocked comments and trying to make sense of what just happened.

I see the crumpled yellow paper on the floor next to me, where Manton must've dropped it. It's a very old ticket to a game, Yankees vs. Red Sox, opening day 1971. Manton must've been just a kid when he went to that game. Maybe even his first game ever.

I get myself untangled from the overturned chairs and stand up, finally looking over at Livvie. She gives me two thumbs up. I smile back, but I'm sad inside my happy. Uncle Luke pats me on the back.

I make my way over to Manton's father and hold out that old ticket. He gives me the dirtiest look I've ever gotten. But he takes the ticket.

And walks out the door.

EPILOGUE

T heo and the Lakers are about to win the Fall Ball Championship, when this amazing kid from West Austin Little League hits a grand slam in the bottom of the last inning. Theo looks disappointed for about twenty seconds, until news of a giant cookie cake starts to spread. Livvie made it, and she's decorated it with every player's name. And age.

Livvie gets a little icing on her WHS Volleyball sweatshirt as she cuts pieces of cookie cake for each boy. And each sibling. And each parent. Arnie and Zach give a joint speech about the fall season's highlights and they say something special about each boy on the team. It *is* kind of amazing to think about – in less than six months, the Lakers have gone from knowing nothing about baseball to being one of the best coach-pitch teams in the city. And they had fun doing it.

I drag over these two gigantic coolers I brought and get the kids' attention. I say I'm proud of all their hard work and I have a surprise for them, then I step back and open the coolers. Hundreds of water balloons are in each. It took me hours of filling and tying, but watching the realization sweep over the boys' faces makes it all worthwhile.

It doesn't take long for a full-fledged water balloon war to break out. Livvie gets me right in the chest and when I retaliate, she catches the balloon I throw at her! Whoever heard of catching one? Then she throws it right back at me, and my tshirt is soaked in back as well as front.

Finally the players head home with their families, slightly damp and full of chocolate chips. Livvie and I walk all over the field picking up tiny fragments of exploded latex balloon. I guess I hadn't really thought that part through, but Livvie is adamant that a bird might eat these and die, so we have to pick up every single one. My mom and dad wait in the Prius, working the New York Times Crossword together. They have added another bumpersticker: WELTON BASEBALL.

I follow the trail of popped balloons all the

way to the outfield. My mind wanders to my own fall ball schedule, and Welton's scrimmage against St. Anthony's coming up this week. Ash didn't get the head varsity position at Welton, but they did wind up hiring him for the JV team. The varsity coach is a guy named Zoiciejowski, and I may not be spelling that correctly. As the matter of fact, it would pretty much be a miracle if I were spelling it right. The guys all call him Coach Zee, and he moved here from Houston when he got the job. Ash is happy just to be on the staff, and of course I'm glad he's there – because I'm on the Welton JV along with Butch and Louie. Bellows and most of the other guys from the Texas Blaze were placed on the freshman team, but at least they are winning. Making JV seemed real exciting at first, but our fall ball record is 2-4 so far. And the game against St. Anthony's is going to be tough, especially since both Billy D and Julio got scholarships to play there. Turns out Mr. Loezier loves Julio even though Julio always talks back to him. Go figure.

Coach Manton wound up moving to California, where he got a job as a statistician on his old semi-pro team, the San Luis Obispo Blues. You can look him up on their website, under the staff page. There's a little bio of him, and in the photo he's wearing his Texas Blaze cap. It makes me feel funny to look at that, since the team doesn't exist anymore. My mom says the town where he's living is this cool little beach community, perfect for retiring.

"You missed one!" Livvie walks up behind me and points to a lone shredded balloon.

"Look what I found." I turn – and show her what was left in the bottom of the cooler. One last water balloon.

"No way..." She starts backing away from me.

"Yes way."

I run after her, but she's tough to catch.

I'm in no hurry.